A GUIDE TO THE
OLYMPIC GAMES
AND
LONDON 2012

BY
MAURICE CROW
AND JULIET MORRIS

Wharncliffe Books

First published in Great Britain in 2012
By Wharncliffe Books
an imprint of
Pen and Sword Books Ltd
47 Church Street
Barnsley
South Yorkshire S70 2AS

Reprinted 2012

ISBN 978 1 84563 149 9

Printed and bound in England
by CPI Group (UK) Ltd,
Croydon, CR0 4YY

Typeset in Helvetica Light by
Chic Media Ltd

Pen & Sword Books Ltd incorporates the imprints of
Pen & Sword Aviation, Pen & Sword Family History, Pen & Sword Maritime,
Pen & Sword Military, Pen & Sword Discovery, Wharncliffe Local History,
Wharncliffe True Crime, Wharncliffe Transport, Pen & Sword Select,
Pen & Sword Military Classics, Leo Cooper, Remember When,
The Praetorian Press, Seaforth Publishing and Frontline Publishing

For a complete list of Pen and Sword titles please contact
Pen and Sword Books Limited
47 Church Street, Barnsley, South Yorkshire, S70 2AS, England
E-mail: enquiries@pen-and-sword.co.uk
Website: www.pen-and-sword.co.uk

CONTENTS

CHAPTER **1**

The Early Years

At the Opening Ceremony of each Olympic Games one athlete, chosen to represent all competitors, takes the following oath: "In the name of all the competitors I promise that we shall take part in these Olympic Games, respecting and abiding by the rules which govern them, in the true spirit of sportsmanship, for the glory of sport and the honour of our teams."

The Olympic Oath was first voiced publicly in 1920 but the ideals it espouses go back almost 3,000 years. According to legend, the ancient Games were founded by Heracles (known to the Romans as Hercules), a son of Zeus. The Olympian Games were the most famous of the four ancient Games – the others being the Isthmian, Pythian and Nemean – and were named after the location in which they were held: Olympia in south-west Greece, Zeus's most important shrine. Archaeologists have demonstrated that the Olympics date back to the second millennium before Christ, but the very first gathering for which there are written records was in 776 BC.

In that year a naked runner, Koroibus, won the main event, known as the stade, a run of approximately 192 metres (210 yards). This made Koroibus, a humble local baker from Elis, the very first Olympic champion in history. Other early victors included a cowherd and a goatherd. Their prize was an olive wreath. In those days the Games were strictly for men, who competed naked or wearing only a thong. For this reason, women were banned, even as spectators – although teenage girls were later allowed to compete in separate, limited races, wearing short tunics with their right breasts exposed.

We know that from at least 776BC the Games were held every Olympiad, a four-year period used in the Greek calendar. During the spring of the chosen year messengers were despatched to all the principal city-states urging them to send their finest athletes. They could be rich or poor but had to be of Greek descent and classed as men of honour. Those who returned successful with a prize of an olive wreath could expect to be feted for the rest of their days, eulogised by poets and offered an allowance from state coffers. The most successful Olympian of these times was Milo of Croton, an associate of Pythagoras, who won five men's wrestling titles between 536 and 520BC.

The ancient Olympian Games grew and continued to be played for more than 1,000 years. During the first 300 centuries of its recorded history, the events were contained within a single day. In 472BC it was expanded into a five-day event beginning with a full day of sacrificial worship to Zeus. The programme of events included boxing, wrestling and a fighting discipline called the pancratium. Boxing was challenging enough, the pugilists progressing from gloves of soft leather strips to ones of tough hide weighted with lead. The pancratium was still more demanding, the fight ending only when one battered contender accepted humiliating defeat.

Sprinting events were considered the most prestigious but some other contests required a degree of wealth on the part of competitors. One test involved racing in full body armour. In the equestrian events the contenders had to provide their own horses. There was also a pentathlon, comprised of sprinting, wrestling, long jump, javelin-throwing and discus-hurling. The discus was oval-shaped and made of bronze, while the standard javelin technique involved a strap wound around the shaft that was ripped downwards at the moment of delivery to give greater distance and accuracy.

The pagan aspects of the ancient Games were its downfall. Roman emperors, having adopted Christianity, began to look with disfavour upon Greeks worshiping their gods of old. Theodosius I, the last of his kind to rule over a united east-west Roman Empire, finally banned all forms of pagan worship in 391AD. Three years later he abolished the Games.

The sporting ideals that had flourished in Ancient Greece died and remained moribund for more than a millennium, through the Dark Ages and the Mediaeval Period. It was not until the early nineteenth century that European aristocrats, schooled in the classics and enticed by the Greek ethos of mind and body in harmony, were drawn to pastimes such as fencing and tennis. A sporting renaissance spread from the nobility to the new middle classes.

A restoration of Olympian athleticism needed only a catalyst – and that came from one man. The father of the modern Olympic Games, Baron Pierre de Coubertin, was born in Paris on 1 January 1863, a member of an old aristocratic French family. From his teen years he was fascinated by classical Greek architecture and ideology. He read how, 100 years earlier, British scientist Richard Chandler had discovered the location of ancient Olympia. And when, between 1875 and 1881, German archaeologist Ernst Curtius uncovered the actual remains of Olympia in the Greek Peloponesse, De Courbetin was enthralled. Curtius himself suggested reviving the Games there but Greece already played host to the popular Pan-Hellenic Games, launched in 1859.

De Coubertin switched the emphasis. Lauding the "noble and chivalrous character" of physical exercise, he saw the global scope of the new Games and set about devising an international sporting event expressed by means of fair competition between nations with equal opportunity for all contestants. The amateur ideal was a prerequisite – and the notion of athletes reaping commercial rewards for their achievements was anathema to him.

As he later declared: "I shall burnish a flabby and cramped youth, its body and its character, by sport, its risks, even its excesses. All this is to be for everyone, with no discrimination on account of birth, caste, financial standing or occupation."

De Courbetin penned articles, lobbied the authorities and held numerous public meetings with the stated aim of "re-establishing the Olympic Games to ennoble and strengthen sports and to assure their independence and durability and, moreover, to allow them better to fulfil an educational role which was their duty in the modern world". This, he later wrote, would be "for the glorification of the individual athlete, whose existence is necessary for the physical activities of the multitude, and whose prowess is essential to continuing general emulation".

Finally, at a Paris conference on 23 June 1894, (regarded as 'founder's day' of the Olympic community), de Courbetin won the unanimous support of the delegates of twelve countries to reconvene the Games in Athens in 1896. He was authorised to form an International Olympic Committee (Comité Internationale Olympique) whose constitution was strangely based on that of Britain's Henley Royal Regatta.

A Greek, Demetrious Vikelas, was chosen as the IOC's first president, and an early move by that nation was to build a permanent venue for the Games on its own soil. The plan was voted down as being against the principles of international partnership. De Coubertin, who initially acted as the committee's secretary general, took over the IOC's presidency from 1896 until 1925.

The enthusiasm of the fledgling IOC and de Courbetin's own idealism were not enough to ensure success, however. The first modern Games could so easily have been a disaster but for the financial backing of Crown Prince Constantine of Greece, who established a fund-raising committee, and of Greek benefactor George Averoff, who paid for the refurbishment of a major stadium. Thus, in Athens on 6 April 1896, King George of Greece opened the first Olympic Games of modern times in front of an audience of 60,000. Some 200 men from fourteen countries competed in forty-three events. Most were Greek citizens but many international competitors arrived in Athens, having paid their own way to enter the history-making event.

In addition to track and field, there also featured gymnastics, wrestling, fencing, weightlifting, cycling, shooting, swimming and tennis. Because of a lack of entrants, both the scheduled soccer and cricket tournaments had to be cancelled. And bad weather caused the abandonment of the rowing and sailing competitions. The first champion of the modern Olympics was an American, James Brendan Connolly, who won the triple jump.

It was the final event, however, that produced the most popular winner. Greek runner Spyridon Louis won the first modern marathon. The legendary 26-mile run from Marathon to Athens had been made by a herald to announce victory in the battle of Marathon in 490BC. The idea of recreating the event in commemoration of the heroic feat had been proposed by a French archaeologist, Michel Breal. That the recreated race should have been won by a poor water carrier from an Athens suburb made Spyridon Louis a national hero.

The Athens Games of 1896 were voted a success by all who participated. There was no pot of gold for the participants, however – indeed, no gold medals. Winners were presented with an olive branch, a certificate, and a silver medal. The runners-up received a laurel sprig and a copper medal.

Athens was an encouraging debut for the de Courbetin dream. But it was a false start. The 1900 Games in Paris (24 countries, 95 events,

THE EARLY YEARS

997 athletes) were notable for being the first to allow women competitors – though only twenty-two of them and in limited events, like golf and tennis. The Games were also notable for their poor organisation, the sporting championships being piggy-backed on to the city's World's Fair and being spread over five months. The result was a lack of excitement among both athletes and spectators – of whom there were disappointingly few.

The hesitant start to the sporting century continued with the 1904 Games in St Louis, Missouri (12 countries, 91 events, 651 athletes, six of them women), which was also linked to an international fair and dragged on from July to November. Even the medals bore the words 'Universal Exhibition' on the front and 'Olympiad' on the back. Just as in Paris, the crowds stayed away.

Back in 1901 the IOC had ignored de Courbetin's entreaties and decided to stage Games biannually, with Athens hosting every two years and other cities taking the intervening years. The result was a return to Athens for the 1906 Games, which proved unexpectedly successful after the debacles of Paris and St Louis. Medals in gold, silver and bronze were awarded. These interim or 'Intercalated' Games were later downgraded and the experiment was dropped.

It is a surprise to many outside the world of sport that Britain's 2012 Olympic Games mark the capital's third role as host. In 1908 London came to the rescue at short notice following Rome's withdrawal because of the crippling cost of the 1906 eruption of Mount Vesuvius. These Games of the IV Olympiad (22 countries, 110 events, 2,008 athletes, 37 of them women), opened in the White City Stadium by King Edward VII, were staged purely as a sporting event and not merely as a side-show to a world exhibition.

The West London venue, built for the Franco-British exhibition earlier that year, had a running track, a velodrome and a large swimming pool. It attracted crowds of 100,000, who saw the emergence of major sporting stars. Most successful were British swimmer Henry Taylor (400 metres, 1500 metres and 4 x 200 metres freestyle) and American athlete Melvin Sheppard (800 metres, 1500 metres and relay), each of whom won three gold medals. There were, however, unsavoury accusations against Britain of home bias from representatives of five countries, most volubly the United States.

One of the most memorable occurrences, however, was the sad failure of an utterly exhausted Italian, Dorando Pietri, to win the

Marathon. On entering the stadium, he astonished 90,000 spectators by turning right instead of left – then fell exhausted to the ground. He was helped to the finishing line before collapsing once again and being stretchered away. His hugely popular 'win' was withdrawn after a US objection forced a doctor's ruling that Pietri could not have completed the race unaided, victory thereby passing to America's John Hayes.

An enduring motto that has been handed down to athletes for over a century was first voiced in London in 1908: "The important thing in the Olympic Games is not winning but taking part." Although often attributed to Baron de Courbertin, it is actually based on words used in a sermon by the Bishop of Central Pennsylvania, Ethelbert Talbot, during an Olympic service at St Paul's Cathedral on 19 July. His full text was: "The most important thing in the Olympic Games is not to win but to take part, just as the most important thing in life is not the triumph but the struggle. The essential thing is not to have conquered but to have fought well."

It was not until Stockholm in 1912 that the Olympics notched up a universally acclaimed success (28 countries, 102 events, 2,407 athletes including 48 women). The Swedish hosts ensured that events ran smoothly, making the Games of the V Olympiad a model for the future. For the first time there were athletes representing every continent. Women were allowed to challenge in more sports, principally in the pool. Another innovation was the photo-finish for track and field events and the introduction of the electronic timer – though only as a back-up to the trusty stopwatch.

The American Jim Thorpe became one of the first true superstars of the modern Games by winning both the pentathlon and decathlon. Tragically, the following year he was stripped of his medals after the IOC decided that his amateur status was flawed by the revelation that he had received payment as a baseball player in his youth. Thorpe died in 1953 but it was not until 1982 that he was rehabilitated and his medals restored to his family.

The Games of the VI Olympiad had been due to take place in Berlin. They became an instant casualty of World War I – and many of the young men who had performed so magnificently in London and Stockholm now fell on the killing fields of France and Belgium. But even though the Berlin Games had been cancelled, their designation as the VI Olympiad was not passed on – so that the first post-war Games became the VII Olympics, staged in 1920. They were awarded to Antwerp, Belgium, itself ravaged by the conflict.

THE EARLY YEARS

The Belgians won praise for organising the Games at such short notice. The event was marked by a requiem Mass for the war dead, and the IOC barred entrants from the defeated powers: Germany, Austria, Hungary, Bulgaria and Turkey. Although battered Belgium did its best, the Games (29 countries, 154 events, 2,626 athletes including 65 women) were marked by low attendances. Antwerp did provide some powerful symbolic legacies for the movement, however.

The Olympic Oath was first voiced in 1920 by Belgian fencer and water polo player Victor Boin. The stirring words are still repeated today by a single sportsman representing the host nation on behalf of all competitors. The Olympic Motto 'Citius, Altius, Fortius' (Swifter, Higher, Stronger), devised by a Domincan monk, Father Henri Didon, also made its first appearance at the 1920 Games. Pigeons or doves, which had been first released at the opening ceremony of 1896, were reintroduced as a symbol of peace in 1920 and have subsequently become a regular feature of every host's ceremonial.

The other enduring symbol first witnessed at Antwerp was a large white banner bearing the five interlaced Olympic rings of blue, yellow, black, green and red, symbolising the five continents. De Coubertin had found this emblem at Delphi in 1913 and decided that the colours would match those in the flags of every nation represented. He had presented the flag to the Olympic movement on its 20th anniversary but it was not until 1920 that it became the official symbol of the Games. The actual standard that flew for the first time in Antwerp was produced by the Belgian Olympic Committee. Made of embroidered satin, it would be flown at every Games until 1988, when it would be replaced by a replica made in Korean silk.

The indefatigable de Coubertin had shouldered much of the administrative burden of the IOC for a quarter of a century. Until the First World War, the headquarters had been his own Paris home, but when he enlisted in the French army in 1916, he temporarily passed the presidency to a Swiss, Baron Godefroy de Blonay, and the organisation relocated to Switzerland – a logical move since de Coubertin had long wished to base the IOC in a neutral state. With de Courbetin back in charge after the war, the IOC in 1922 established its HQ in a manor called 'Mon Repos' in the Swiss city of Lausanne. The organisation remained there until 1968, when the need for more space required a further move to the Chateau de Vidy on the shores of Lake Geneva.

It was from Switzerland that the IOC organised the next Games, a return to Paris in 1924 (44 nations, 126 events, 3,089 athletes including 135 women) that gave the city a chance to make amends for its faltering performance in 1900. This time the French made every effort to ensure the Games ran smoothly. Money was lavished on the facilities. An Olympic Village was built to house the athletes, a 500 metre track was laid at a new track-and-field stadium near Colombes, and a 10,000-seater swimming arena built at Tourelles.

For the first time, fans listening to their wireless sets at home could follow the action through live radio transmissions. And action there was in one of the greatest sporting dramas of all time. For the 100 metres sprint crown, America's Charley Paddock was favourite but two Britons, Eric Liddell and Harold Abrahams, challenged his supremacy during preliminary runs. When it came to the final, however, Liddell, a devout Christian, refused to race because it was held on a Sunday and instead went to preach at a church in Paris. Abrahams, who was Jewish, went on to win a gold medal, covering the 100 metres in 10.6 seconds. The story of the British pair's differing paths to glory was retold in the film 'Chariots Of Fire'.

While the summertime Olympics grew in stature, a lengthy campaign by winter sports lovers had gathered momentum. Figure skating had been included in the London Games of 1908 and ice hockey had been added in Antwerp in 1920 but it was not until 1924 that the IOC dropped its resistance and staged an 'International Winter Sports Week' at the French resort of Chamonix. So successful was it that a year later the first Winter Olympic Games were announced, to be held in the same year as the next Summer Games. (The full story of this is covered in a further Chapter.)

Around the time of the 1925 authorisation of a separate Winter Olympics, the ageing Baron Pierre de Courbetin stepped down and was replaced as IOC president by Belgian Henri de Baillet-Latour, whose tenure would last until 1942.

A further change of heart by the IOC came at this time with the announcement that women would at last be allowed to enter track and field competitions – something de Courbetin had fought against. Nevertheless, the next Summer Games, held in Amsterdam in 1928 (46 countries, 109 events, 2,883 athletes, all but 277 of them men), still barred women from competing in races longer than 200 metres, a ruling that endured until 1960. De Coubertin was not there to witness the female newcomers. Illness kept the sixty-five-year-old from the Games, the first he had missed since 1908.

THE EARLY YEARS

Another innovation at Amsterdam was the introduction of the Olympic torch. It was a belief of the ancient Greeks that fire had sacred qualities given to humanity by the god Prometheus, so torch relays were part of their Games rituals – a sacred flame lit in Olympia at the altar of Zeus. In 1928, at the top of a tower within Amsterdam's magnificent Olympic Stadium, a flame was lit for the first time in the modern Games and remained lit throughout. (At this time the Olympic torch relay had not yet been invented.)

The most successful athlete at Amsterdam was Finnish runner Paavo Nurmi, who at his third Games picked up his tenth, eleventh and twelfth Olympic medals. Another crowd pleaser was American swimmer Johnny Weissmuller, who went on to become the most famous of all movie Tarzans. Germany was allowed to re-enter the Games after a sixteen-year exile and its team won ten golds, still far short of the USA's twenty-two.

The 1932 Los Angeles Games (37 nations, 117 events, 1,332 athletes including 126 women) were muted because of the Great Depression. So soon after the 1929 Wall Street crash, sports budgets were a low priority even by the host nation. Nevertheless, a festive atmosphere was created, particularly at the opening ceremony where a 100,000 crowd gathered in the Coliseum to be entertained by 3,500 musicians. The Games were the first to take place over sixteen days. Other innovations included the use of a three-level podium for the medal ceremonies, automatic timing for track events and the photo-finish. Male athletes were accommodated in a single Olympic village, following up an idea first tried at Athens in 1906.

The LA Games were marred by controversy even before they opened. The Finnish runner Paavo Nurmi, aged thirty-five, had hoped to cap his career by capturing the marathon gold medal to add to his other honours, which included nine Olympic golds, three silvers and twenty-five official world records. But the IOC banned him for violation of amateur regulations – on the grounds that he had claimed expenses for travel to sporting meetings.

The last Games before World War II were held in Berlin in 1936 (49 countries, 129 events, 3,963 athletes, 331of them women) and were opened by Chancellor Adolf Hitler. They were judged a success – despite the overt manipulation of the Olympics as a publicity platform for the glorification of the Nazi regime.

Berlin had been due to host the Games back in 1916 but, ironically, it was World War I that shelved that plan. The restoration of the German capital as venue was a popular choice at the time the decision was made – before Hitler came to power. But in the run-up to the 1936 event protests grew. In the United States Jewish groups in particular called for a boycott. US Olympic officials began to have second thoughts but Avery Brundage, chairman of the US National Olympic Committee and future IOC president, argued that the Germans had proved themselves adept at organising the previous Winter Games at Garmisch-Partenkirchen and the Americans finally voted by fifty-eight to fifty-six to send a team.

So the Berlin Games went ahead – marked by some remarkable moments and some vital innovations. The Games of the XI Olympiad were the first to be broadcast on television, relayed via closed circuit to the city's cinemas. But more significantly it was the first to introduce the ritual of the Olympic torch relay.

The idea is attributed to Carl Diem, chairman of the Games organising committee, who suggested that a flame be lit in Olympia and brought by a series of relay runners from Greece and across Europe to Germany. Thus, in July 1936, the Olympic torch, sparked alight by the sun in front of the Temple of Hera, was relayed by 3,075 torchbearers to the German capital where, on 1 August in Berlin's impressive 100,000-seat Olympic stadium, a cauldron was lit that would burn for the duration of the competition.

Much to the delight of Hitler and his swastika-waving spectators, the German team was overall winner of the Games, with thirty-two golds ahead of America's twenty-four. But it was as well that the US team came to Berlin – because it allowed one man's achievement to make a mockery of the Nazi creed of Aryan superiority. That hero was, of course, Jesse Owens.

This grandson of slaves proved himself one of the all-time greats of athletics by winning the 100 metres sprint in 10.3 seconds, matching the Olympic record, setting a new 200 metres world and Olympic record of 20.7 seconds, winning a new Olympic record with a long jump of 8.05 metres and being a member of the world record-beating 100 metres relay team. Ordinary Germans cheered Owens' achievements but, infamously, an angry Hitler refused to celebrate the awarding of four gold medals to a black winner.

Owens' spectacular rebuttal of the Nazi creed overshadows that of one other hero of Berlin. Owens' long-jump opponent Luz Long, a fair-haired blue-eyed German, befriended his black opponent and encouraged him when he was in danger of going out through fouls during the qualifying round. Long, who was first to congratulate the American after his win, was later lauded by Owens in these words: "You can melt down all my medals and cups and they would be just a plating on the 22 carat friendship I felt for Luz Long at that moment."

So, as the world lurched again towards war, the enduring image of the Berlin Games was of a heroic black champion and a defiant white rival ignoring the poisoned politics of their Nazi hosts to support so publicly the Olympic Ideal.

Less than a year after the closing ceremony under the swirling swastika banners in Berlin's Olympic Stadium, the outbreak of the Sino-Japanese war meant that the XII Summer Games, due to be staged in Japan in 1940, were transferred to Helsinki. The Winter Games, also awarded to Japan, were transferred first to St Moritz and later to Garmisch Partenkirchen. Both switches were, of course, soon invalidated in 1939 by the Soviet invasion of Finland and the declaration of war between the Allies and Germany. The 1944 Summer Games of the XIII Olympiad scheduled for London and the Winter Games planned for Cortina d'Ampezzo were also cancelled.

In 1944 a ceremony was held in neutral Switzerland to mark the fiftieth anniversary of the Olympic revival. Only a handful of IOC members turned up. Yet World War II failed to extinguish the Olympic flame. In 1940 a group of Californian athletes and coaches decided to stage their own 'mini-Olympics' at the Los Angeles Coliseum. The event was titled 'Champions of 1940', a track and field meet, with proceeds going to the Finnish Relief Fund to help Finns driven from their country by the Soviet Union's invasion. Fittingly the Finn Taisto Maki, the world's foremost two-miler, was the star name.

As the world struggled out of conflict and into a period of Cold War suspicion and enmity, the International Olympic Committee, under the Swede Sigfrid Edstrom, elected president in 1946, began to evaluate its previous pledges to possible Olympic host nations. It became obvious that first-class athletic performances could not disguise the fact that the Olympics were in danger of being misused by post-war nations in their struggle for prestige.

It was fortunate, therefore, that one city came forward to demonstrate how sport could reunite a world torn apart by war. The Games of the XIV Olympiad resumed in 1948 ... once again with London as proud host.

CHAPTER 2

1948: London

29 July – 14 August

Games of the XIV Olympiad

Countries participating: 59

Athletes participating:
4,104 (3,714 men, 390 women)

Events: 136 in 19 sports

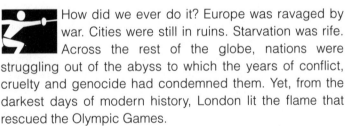 How did we ever do it? Europe was ravaged by war. Cities were still in ruins. Starvation was rife. Across the rest of the globe, nations were struggling out of the abyss to which the years of conflict, cruelty and genocide had condemned them. Yet, from the darkest days of modern history, London lit the flame that rescued the Olympic Games.

The last Games had, notoriously, been held in Berlin in 1936 when the Olympic ideal had been corrupted and turned into a propaganda exercise by the Nazi regime. After that, two Olympic years, 1940 and 1944, had been wiped from the calendar by the Second World War. London had been due to host the latter event, which is why the capital was now offered the Games of the XIV Olympiad for 1948.

But surely it was an impossibility? London was on its knees. Could not the one rich, surviving nation not rescue the Games? The United States did indeed consider offering to stage them – until it became obvious that it would be unreasonable for countries impoverished by war to be asked

to send their teams across the Atlantic to compete. And it quickly became clear that no-one else was willing to make the necessary arrangements to host such a monumental undertaking. So London valiantly agreed. It would be the second occasion that London had hosted the Olympics, the city previously being the venue in 1908. At that time the capital had been at the height of imperial power, hope and glory; Forties Britain was a very different land.

After the VE and VJ Day celebrations had died down and sombre reality set in, there remained only two years to meet the deadline of restoring the Games to their regular schedule. Yet Britain was still in the grip of wartime rationing with food, fuel and building materials in desperately short supply. London, blitzed and battered for five years, had ended up broke and with more bomb sites than usable sporting venues. One iconic stadium had survived, however… Wembley. And it was in the shadows of those famous 'Twin Towers' that the major events of what became known as 'the Austerity Games' were to be held.

That there was even a Wembley as a workable stadium was largely due to one ingenious entrepreneur, Arthur Elvin, an ex-scrap dealer and cigarette kiosk owner who ended up buying the stadium after it was deemed 'financially unviable' following the British Empire Exhibition there in 1924. Ten years later he opened a new indoor Sports Arena and Empire Pool alongside the main stadium. Used for the 1934 British Empire Games, it was later renamed the Wembley Arena.

In 1946 Sir Arthur Elvin, who was knighted that year for his services to sport, rose to the challenge of creating a modern facility suitable for the post-war period. Firstly, to cope with the crowds, a new road was created from a specially enlarged Wembley Park tube station to the stadium. It was called Olympic Way, although sports fans have always known it as Wembley Way. The Wembley local authorities realised that hosting the Olympics would have to be non-profit making, but still offered to bear the £120,000 cost of creating the new route. For work inside the stadium itself a special Act of Parliament was required to make structural changes, build modern dressing rooms, recondition the terraces, widen corridors and improve car parking facilities.

At pitch level substantial reconstruction was also required. The running track, first laid in 1923, had been buried beneath a greyhound course. With only three weeks to go before the opening ceremony, 100 workmen began the task of recreating a world-class running surface, digging down to the foundations, laying 800 tons of cinders and using scientific measuring equipment to set levels and distances. The excellence of their work in creating that brand new track resulted in seventeen world and Olympic records being broken during the course of the Games.

Because of food shortages and rationing it was agreed that Britain should not bear full responsibility for feeding the athletes. So the visiting teams actually arrived with their own supplies. Any surplus food was then donated to local hospitals. Athletes were allowed to break rationing rules, being given increased rations to match the intake of British dockers and miners – 5,467 calories a day as opposed to the normal 2,600 calories.

Housing the contestants was also hand-to-mouth. No Olympic Village was erected, the athletes instead being accommodated in schools, military camps and private homes. The bulk of the male athletes were housed at RAF and Army camps in Uxbridge, West Drayton and Richmond, and the women in dormitories at women's colleges, such as Southlands in south-west London.

Other sites were earmarked for sporting activities far beyond Wembley, including: Empress Hall, Earl's Court (boxing preliminaries, wrestling, weightlifting, gymnastics), Harringay Arena (basketball), Royal Regatta Course, Henley-on-Thames (canoeing, rowing), Herne Hill Velodrome (track cycling), Windsor Great Park (cycling road race), Central Stadium, Aldershot Military HQ (equestrian), Tweseldown Racecourse, Hampshire (equestrian), Finchley Pool (water polo preliminaries), National Rifle Association Ranges, Bisley (shooting), and the waters off Torbay (yachting). Football preliminaries were held at: Arsenal Stadium, Highbury; Crystal Palace's Selhurst Park; Craven Cottage, Fulham; Goldstone Ground, Brighton; Champion Hill, Dulwich; Green Pond Road Stadium, Walthamstow; White Hart Lane, Tottenham; Brentford's Griffin Park; and Ilford FC ground. And the hockey preliminaries were held at: Lyons' Sports Club, Sudbury; Guinness Sports Club, Park Royal and Polytechnic Sports Ground, Chiswick.

When the Games officially opened on 29 July, in the presence of the IOC's newly-elected Swedish president Sigfrid Edstrom, London had prepared for the arrival of teams from fifty-nine nations comprising more than 4,000 competitors. Wembley Stadium itself would see thirty-three track and field events being contested by more than 800 athletes from fifty-three of those countries. Significant absentees were Germany and Japan, the aggressors of World War II, who were not invited to participate. Significant entrants included competitors from countries that now found themselves under Communist governments.

A GUIDE TO THE OLYMPIC GAMES AND LONDON 2012

An impressively vast timber scoreboard had been constructed and a concrete platform laid to house the Olympic Flame. On a brilliantly sunny 29 July, King George VI, who officially opened the Games, Queen Elizabeth, and other members of the Royal Family – plus 85,000 commoners – watched an impressive ceremony, serenaded by the massed bands of the Brigade of Guards. Seven thousand pigeons, symbolising doves of peace, were released and a twenty-one-gun salute was followed by the arrival of the Olympic flame, borne aloft by Cambridge Blue John Mark. And that Olympic torch was very different to every other in the history of the Games – as is explained in the panel on p27.

The welcome speech to the athletes was given by the Games chairman, Lord Burghley, president of the Amateur Athletics Association and a gold medal winner at the 1928 Olympics. He set the tone by urging them to "keen but friendly rivalry". London, he said, represented "a warm flame of hope for a better understanding in the world which has burned so low".

He added this rallying call: "Your Majesty, the hour has struck. A visionary dream has today become a glorious reality. At the end of the worldwide struggle in 1945, many institutions and associations were found to have withered and only the strongest had survived. How, many wondered, had the great Olympic Movement prospered?"

The answer might well have already been provided by the century's early pioneers under Baron Pierre de Courbetin, founder of the International Olympic Committee. These were the first Games to be held following his death in 1937, but the noble sentiments first expressed in 1908 were particularly pertinent in a Europe so recently ravaged by war: "The most important thing in the Olympic Games is not winning but taking part. The essential thing is not to have conquered but to have fought well."

And so it proved. The first post-war Games were a triumph in every way: a celebration of peace and a symbol of how sport could unite a war-weary world. The era of professionalism, or even semi-professionalism, had not yet dawned and the events in and around London were conducted in the most innocent and honest sporting spirit.

Many names unknown to the British public became overnight heroes. Some sports were also novelties. A new sporting body, the Union Internationale de Modern Pentathlon, was founded during the Games, on 3 August. The modern pentathlon, made up of five sports, was contested over six days. And a thirty-three-year-old Swedish artillery captain, Willie Grut, astounded the organisers by scoring the most decisive victory in the history of the event by finishing first in three of the five disciplines: horse riding, fencing and swimming. Not only that but he finished fifth in pistol shooting and eighth in 4,000 metres cross-country running. It was a confirmation of his all-round sporting abilities for earlier that year, Grut had finished second in a demonstration pentathlon at the St Moritz Winter Olympics, consisting of equestrian, fencing, downhill skiing and cross-country skiing. He later became Sweden's national team manager.

The decathlon provided an equal surprise. It was won by Bob Mathias of the United States at the age of just seventeen. He became the youngest ever Olympic gold medallist in athletics, an even more remarkable achievement given that he had only taken up the event earlier that year at the instigation of his high school coach. When asked how he would celebrate, the Californian teenager replied: "I'll start shaving, I guess." Mathias went on to win all eleven decathlons he contested over the next twelve years, including the retention of his title at the Helsinki Games in 1952.

Back at Wembley drama surrounded the end of the marathon as the first man to enter the stadium, Belgium's Etienne Gailly, stumbled into view exhausted and almost unable to run. As the crowds willed him on, Argentinia's Delfo Cabrera and Britain's Tom Richards passed him, with Cabrera winning the gold, Richards the silver and Gailly struggling across the line to take the bronze.

A seemingly more effortless performance at Wembley was given by emerging superstar Emil Zatopek, twenty-five, then an unknown Czechoslovakian army officer who smashed the world 10,000 metres record by twelve seconds and went on to dominate distance running for many years. He is best known for winning three gold medals at the 1952 Olympics.

Another Czech hit the headlines in 1948 – but only in Britain and for a very different reason. Marie Provaznikova, the fifty-seven-year-old president of the International Gymnastics Federation, refused to return home to Prague, citing "lack of freedom" after her homeland was swallowed up by the Soviets. This made London the first Olympics to see a political defection.

Another kind of breakthrough in London came in the high jump when America's Alice Coachman became the first black woman to win an Olympic gold medal in track and field with a leap of 1.68 metres. Coachman had dominated this discipline since 1939 but had been unable to demonstrate her Olympic supremacy because of the war. In 1948 she made her winning jump (then marked as 5ft 6¹/sin) on her first try. Her unlucky rival, Great Britain's Dorothy Tyler, matched it but only on her second try.

A pioneer of Caribbean athletics, Arthur Wint became the first Jamaican to win an Olympic gold medal. Wint had come to Britain during the war and served as a flying officer in the RAF. He went on to study as a doctor and ran simply for enjoyment, appearing at London's White City stadium to excite the crowds with his 440 yards and 880 yards dashes. But it was at Wembley that he made his mark internationally. He took the silver medal behind America's Mal Whitfield in the 800 metres, then went on to win the 400 metres ahead of his more fancied Jamaican team-mate Herb McKenley, with Whitfield third. His 46.2 seconds equalled the Olympic record.

Sadly, the twenty-eight-year-old 'Gentle Giant', as he was nicknamed, missed his third medal in the London Games by pulling a muscle in the 4 x 400 metres relay final. Tragedy struck when, seized by cramp, Wint collapsed on the cinder track and his team could not finish. Heroic Dr Wint, who became Jamaican High Commissioner to London from 1974 to 1978, also appeared at the next Olympics in Helsinki, where he took silver in the 800 metres and his team won gold in the 4 x 400 metres relay.

Another competitor of professional distinction was Frenchwoman Micheline Ostermeyer, a highly talented concert pianist whose delicate hands proved versatile at Wembley. The twenty-five-year-old, who graduated from the Conservatoire de Paris with high honours, had spent the war at her family's home in Tunis where she was the star of a classical radio show. But Wembley Stadium saw her most celebrated performance, winning gold medals in both the shot put and discus – despite having picked up a discus for the first time just a few weeks before the event. She also took the bronze at the high jump.

After winning the shot put, Ostermeyer ended the day by performing a Beethoven concert for fellow team members at their headquarters. While continuing her career as a pianist she went on to win twelve French titles. As such a talented all-rounder she would have been a prime candidate for the pentathlon, but the multi-event competition was not added to the Olympic programme until many years later.

Ostermeyer's performance was only overshadowed by that of one other woman in 1948. She, of course, was the legendary Fanny Blankers-Koen who won four gold medals – and could well have won six if she had been encouraged to compete in two other events. The next occasion any woman came close to matching her feat was in 1988 when Florence Griffith Joyner raced to three golds and a silver in Seoul.

Twelve years earlier the Dutch teenager had appeared at the Berlin Olympics where she had finished sixth in the high jump. While there, she had asked Jesse Owens for an autograph. Now, in London, Blankers-Koen matched her hero's achievement. But it had not been an easy path to glory...

Blankers-Koen already held the world record for the 100 yards when Germany invaded Holland in 1940. Suffering under Nazi occupation, she continued to train and compete when opportunity allowed but by the time of the London Games in 1948 there was little indication that this unassuming mother of two would become the heroine of the Austerity Games.

Yet Blankers-Koen, the 'Flying Dutchwoman', won gold medals in the 100 metres, 200 metres, 80 metres hurdles (in which she set a new world record) and 4 x 100 metres relay – four of the only nine events that women could enter at that time. If she had also contested the long jump and high jump she could well have won those as well, because they were both disciplines in which she was the current world record holder. As it transpired the long jump winning mark was far short of her personal best. Incredibly, however, her chances had been dismissed beforehand by Jack Crump, the secretary of the Amateur Athletics Association, who suggested that, at thirty and with two children, she was too old to enter.

After the Games Blankers-Koen arrived home to a rapturous welcome. In sharp contrast to the riches that subsequent female Olympians like Griffith Joyner have earned, Holland's national heroine was rewarded by the city of Amsterdam with a new bicycle. The Flying Dutchwoman, who died in 2004 at the age of eighty-five, never asked for nor expected anything more.

Interviewed at the age of eighty, she said: "With the war so soon over we were surprised but happy that Britain was organising an Olympic Games, but I had no great expectations of it – nor of myself, because I had had two babies during the war.

"I remember the track had been made only weeks before the event. It was cinder and there had been quite a lot of rain, but we were just very happy to be able to run and compete again.

"There was no Olympic village and we girls were housed in a school, six to a room, about half an hour's journey by train from the stadium. We used to walk to the station, wait for a train and then make our own way to Wembley. Now athletes are very well looked after. It is a great commercial business enterprise these days. Back then there was much more in the way of friendship and we were all happy just to be taking part.

"In 1948 no-one ever thought it would be possible to make money from doing something you enjoyed. We were happy to have the opportunity to travel, see interesting places and meet nice people.

"If people can make lots of money from doing something they are good at, then I am pleased for them. But it doesn't mean they are having any more fun than I did when I competed. I think money often brings only pressure, not happiness. I have no regrets because I have my memories and they are worth all the money in the world as far as I'm concerned. Anyway, that bicycle was very good. It lasted me for many years."

Blankers-Koen, whose nickname in Holland was the 'Flying Housewife', added reminiscently: "After the Games I remember thinking how strange that I had made so many people happy. But times were harsh and I think people were just glad of the opportunity to celebrate anything. It made me very proud to know I had been able to bring joy into people's lives."

By the time the London Olympics closed on 14 August, total expenditure on the Austerity Games had amounted to just £600,000 and final accounts showed profits of £10,000. They sound small sums by today's standards but they reflected a different age, different tastes and different values. The Games of the XIV Olympiad had been a remarkable success.

American broadcaster Siegmund Smith summed up the spirit of the day with these words: "I record my genuine admiration for the achievements of the British people, not only in staging the Games but in staging them the way they did. I liked the crowd's behaviour at every event and I admired their sportsmanship."

The final word on the London Games, however, can be left to the unchallengeable heroine of them. Fanny Blankers-Koen once said: "The Olympics are the greatest uniting competition in the world. Every four years people come together from all over the world to compete against each other, meet one another and share their experiences. They don't speak each other's languages but, for a few weeks, they can live together peacefully.

"How different, for instance, my life might have been if others had learned that lesson earlier."

THE 1948 OLYMPIC FLAME

The Olympic torch that entered the Empire Stadium on 29 July differed from all others in the history of the Games by its similarity to a giant sparkler, spewing a trail of thick, white smoke behind it. It was certainly unlike any of the 1,600 torches that had passed the sacred flame on its journey from Olympia to London.

This apparent irreverence had its origin a fortnight earlier when Castleton Knight, legendary producer of Gaumont-British News, was filming the opening sequence for his Technicolor feature 'The XIV Olympiad – The Glory of Sport', hyped at the time as "the greatest combined operation in the history of the British film industry".

The Opening Ceremony Programme simply recorded: "… a fire was lit on an altar erected on the traditional site of the ancient Olympic temple in southern Greece." However, as the solid wax fuel produced a flame that was almost invisible in sunlight, cameraman Stan Sayer adjusted the mix until it glowed with colour and emitted a fine trail of smoke.

What transpired next is revealed by author K Angus Robertson in his biography of Castleton Knight, titled 'Wild Monkey'. Back in England, cameraman Sayer continued experimenting with ways to improve the cinematic look of the Olympic flame using magnesium powder from an RAF flare. The result was a pyrotechnic sacred fire that melted the official aluminium torches, requiring the final torch bearer, John Mark, to circle the track and mount the ramp on the east terrace carrying a much heavier steel version.

This meddling would never be tolerated today but J Arthur Rank had secured the exclusive film rights from the Olympic Games Committee, formed the Olympic Games of 1948 Film Company, and placed his maverick newsreel producer in effective control of all media arrangements, nationally and internationally, a monopoly much resented by his rivals. Knight set up headquarters in his own production village built across the car park in the grounds of the Civic Hall, the hospitality marquee being a magnet for all visiting VIPs and Rank movie stars.

MEDALS TABLE
LONDON 1948 – GAMES OF THE XIV OLYMPIAD
SUMMER OLYMPIC GAMES

Nation	Gold	Silver	Bronze	Total
United States	38	27	19	84
Sweden	16	11	17	44
France	10	6	13	29
Hungary	10	5	12	27
Italy	8	11	8	27
Finland	8	7	5	20
Turkey	6	4	2	12
Czechoslovakia	6	2	3	11
Switzerland	5	10	5	20
Denmark	5	7	8	20
Netherlands	5	2	9	16
Great Britain	3	14	6	23
Argentina	3	3	1	7
Australia	2	6	5	13
Belgium	2	2	3	7
Egypt	2	2	1	5
Mexico	2	1	2	5
South Africa	2	1	1	4
Norway	1	3	3	7
Jamaica	1	2	0	3
Austria	1	0	3	4
India	1	0	0	1
Peru	1	0	0	1
Yugoslavia	0	2	0	2
Canada	0	1	2	3
Portugal	0	1	1	2
Uruguay	0	1	1	2
Ceylon	0	1	0	1
Cuba	0	1	0	1
Spain	0	1	0	1
Trinidad and Tobago	0	1	0	1
South Korea	0	0	2	2

1948: LONDON

Nation	Gold	Silver	Bronze	Total
Panama	0	0	2	2
Brazil	0	0	1	1
Iran	0	0	1	1
Poland	0	0	1	1
Puerto Rico	0	0	1	1

* The authors believe that the medal tables throughout this book are up-to-date. The results have been thoroughly researched but, mainly due to subsequent disputes and disqualifications, there are discrepancies even among official sites.

* The list of sports take into account principal categories, with subsidiary events omitted.

SPORTS - LONDON 1948

Events: 136 in 19 sports – Athletics | Basketball | Boxing | Canoeing | Cycling | Diving | Equestrian | Fencing | Field hockey | Football (soccer) | Gymnastics | Modern pentathlon | Rowing | Sailing | Shooting | Swimming | Water polo | Weightlifting | Wrestling.

CHAPTER 3

1952: Helsinki

19 July – 3 August

Games of the XV Olympiad

Countries participating: 69

Athletes participating:
4,955 (4,436 men, 519 women)

Events: 149 in 19 sports

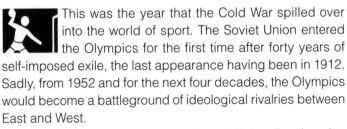

This was the year that the Cold War spilled over into the world of sport. The Soviet Union entered the Olympics for the first time after forty years of self-imposed exile, the last appearance having been in 1912. Sadly, from 1952 and for the next four decades, the Olympics would become a battleground of ideological rivalries between East and West.

A Cold-War atmosphere dominated Finland's otherwise inspiring Games as the Soviets barred the Olympic torch from crossing their territory. They then demanded to segregate their athletes, even suggesting flying them into Finland for specific events. Instead they set up a rival Olympic village for Eastern Bloc countries. While the rest of the world's athletes were based at the official site in the Helsinki suburb of Kapyla, the communist bloc countries established their own village at Otaniemi. At this secluded camp the Soviet team erected a huge scoreboard to highlight the competition between themselves and US athletes. As we shall see, the results were not always to their liking.

Germany and Japan, barred in 1948, were invited to participate. Post-war occupation meant that individual teams represented the western Federal Republic and its small neighbour, the Saarland protectorate, yet-to-be reunited with the rest of West Germany. However, the communist Democratic Republic stayed away, refusing to contribute athletes to a united German team.

A further withdrawal came from the government of the Republic of China (at that time known as Formosa and now as Taiwan) in protest at the acceptance of the communist People's Republic of China. Apart from China other nations making their debut were Ghana (then the Gold Coast), Guatemala, Hong Kong, Indonesia, the Netherlands Antilles, Nigeria, Thailand, the Bahamas and Vietnam. But perhaps the most significant new entry was Israel. The fledgling state had boycotted the 1936 Nazi extravaganza in Berlin and had been embroiled in its own 'war of independence' at the time of the 1948 London Olympics.

Helsinki itself had been allocated the 1940 Olympics after Tokyo pulled out but the occasion was, of course, cancelled by the outbreak of war. Twelve years later, however, the little nation put on an amazing world-class performance. The Finnish capital, with a population of only 367,000, was the smallest city ever to play host. But its citizens were privileged to witness a Games in which the greatest number of world records were broken.

To the delight of the crowds the Olympic flame was lit by two Finnish heroes, runners Paavo Nurmi and Hannes Kolehmainen. Fifty-five-year-old Nurmi, arguably the greatest distance runner in history, lit the flame in the stadium then passed the torch to sixty-two-year-old Kolehmainen, who lit a second flame.

From the start, because of its separatist stance, the focus was on the USSR, which led the medal chart through the early stages with strong showings in track, wrestling and gymnastics. Its first gold medal was won by Nina Romashkova in the women's discus throwing event. Particularly impressive were the women gymnasts, who topped the team competition easily – the first of its eight consecutive gold medals – beginning a winning streak that would last until the break-up of the Soviet Union forty years later.

In Helsinki, however, the scoreboard at Otaniemi showed the US edging them out in the overall medal count. In the closing days American athletes passed the Soviet score, helped by five gold medals from the boxing team. The Americans wound up with seventy-six medals, against the Soviets' seventy-one, and forty golds, against twenty-two for their red rivals.

1952: HELSINKI

Bob Mathias of the United States became the first Olympian to successfully defend his decathlon title, with a total score of 7,887 points. Fellow American Horace Ashenfelter also made headlines – partly because of his career as an FBI agent. Little was expected of him when he was pitched against world record Vladimir Kazantsev of the Soviet Union in the 3,000 metres steeplechase. But when Kazantsev stumbled at the final water jump, the American streaked to victory in a world record 8 minutes 45.4 seconds. A jubilant American press pointed out that it was the first time an FBI agent had been happy to be tailed by a Russian.

The smaller nations enjoyed a successful Games. Hungary, a country of nine million, won forty-two medals, achieving third place behind the US and USSR. Jamaican runners excelled over the 400 metres. And Josy Barthel of Luxembourg upset the forecasters by winning the 1,500 metres – so unexpectedly that the medal ceremony was delayed while the band found the score for his national anthem. Trailing behind Barthel was Britain's Roger Bannister, who returned home vowing to become the first man to break the four-minute mile. He succeeded two years later.

Most successful female athlete was twenty-year-old Marjorie Jackson, known as the Lithgow Flash, who became Australia's first gold medallist when she succeeded the great Fanny Blankers-Koen as the world's fastest woman by winning the 100 metres and 200 metres sprint double. In heats she had set new world records of 11.5 seconds in the 100 metres and 23.4 seconds in the 200 metres. Sadly, the Aussie lost out on the chance of a third gold when she dropped the baton in the 4 x 100 metres relay.

Another superstar in 1952 was Czechoslovakia's Emil Zatopek, otherwise notable for the seemingly agonised grimaces and facial contortions he displayed while competing. Having won the 10,000 metres in London four years earlier, Zatopek excelled himself in Helsinki with an unprecedented triple of the 5,000 metres, 10,000 metres and finally the marathon – in which he had never previously competed. During the course of the race, he shocked the leader, world record holder Jim Peters of Great Britain, by asking him if he thought their pace was too slow. Peters later collapsed with cramp. Within an hour of Zatopek's 5,000 metres victory, his wife Dana also won a gold medal in the javelin.

A rare sour note entered the Games in the boxing ring when Sweden's Ingemar Johansson was disqualified in the heavyweight final for "not trying". Further, his silver medal was withheld for fourteen years.

His victor was America's Floyd Patterson, a tough teen on the streets of Brooklyn who had become known as the 'quiet tiger'. He turned pro after his controversial gold medal middleweight win. Patterson was also the first man to regain the championship when, after losing his title to Johansson in 1959, he knocked out the Swede the following year. The pair struck up a firm friendship, however, and even ran marathons together.

In team games, India won the field hockey for the fifth successive time, the US took the basketball for the third successive time and Hungary won the association football for the first time, with what is still regarded as one of the finest teams ever assembled.

When the Games of the XV Olympiad drew to a close at Helsinki's Olympic Stadium on 3 August, it was universally agreed that the Finns had conducted the most successful Games thus far. During the course of them, the competing athletes, even those separated by enmity and ideology, warmed to each other in sporting fraternity during the course of the events. Nevertheless the confrontational approach of the hard-line Soviet authorities had produced a chill wind from the east that was to blow across Olympic stadia for four decades to come.

MEDALS TABLE
HELSINKI 1952 – GAMES OF THE XV OLYMPIAD
SUMMER OLYMPIC GAMES

Nation	Gold	Silver	Bronze	Total
United States	40	19	17	76
Soviet Union	22	30	19	71
Hungary	16	10	16	42
Sweden	12	13	10	35
Italy	8	9	4	21
Czechoslovakia	7	3	3	13
France	6	6	6	18
Finland	6	3	13	22
Australia	6	2	3	11
Norway	3	2	0	5
Switzerland	2	6	6	14
South Africa	2	4	4	10
Jamaica	2	3	0	5
Belgium	2	2	0	4
Denmark	2	1	3	6
Turkey	2	0	1	3
Japan	1	6	2	9
Great Britain	1	2	8	11
Argentina	1	2	2	5
Poland	1	2	1	4
Canada	1	2	0	3
Yugoslavia	1	2	0	3
Romania	1	1	2	4
Brazil	1	0	2	3
New Zealand	1	0	2	3
India	1	0	1	2
Luxembourg	1	0	0	1
Germany	0	7	17	24
Netherlands	0	5	0	5
Iran	0	3	4	7
Chile	0	2	0	2
Austria	0	1	1	2

Nation	Gold	Silver	Bronze	Total
Lebanon	0	1	1	2
Ireland	0	1	0	1
Mexico	0	1	0	1
Spain	0	1	0	1
South Korea	0	0	2	2
Trinidad and Tobago	0	0	2	2
Uruguay	0	0	2	2
Bulgaria	0	0	1	1
Egypt	0	0	1	1
Portugal	0	0	1	1
Venezuela	0	0	1	1

SPORTS - HELSINKI 1952

Events: 149 in 19 sports – Athletics | Basketball | Boxing | Canoeing | Cycling | Diving | Equestrian | Fencing | Field hockey | Football (soccer) | Gymnastics | Modern pentathlon | Rowing | Sailing | Shooting | Swimming | Water polo | Weightlifting | Wrestling.

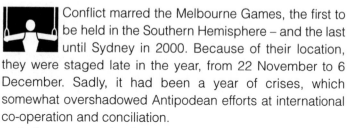

CHAPTER 4

1956: Melbourne

22 November – 8 December

Games of the XVI Olympiad

Countries participating: 67

Athletes participating:
3,155 (2,791 men, 364 women)

Events: 145 in 19 sports

Conflict marred the Melbourne Games, the first to be held in the Southern Hemisphere – and the last until Sydney in 2000. Because of their location, they were staged late in the year, from 22 November to 6 December. Sadly, it had been a year of crises, which somewhat overshadowed Antipodean efforts at international co-operation and conciliation.

In the run-up to the Games the Hungarian uprising against their Soviet masters was brutally crushed. The result was a boycott by Spain, the Netherlands and Switzerland in protest against Russian involvement – although Hungary itself remained represented.

The Suez Crisis earlier in the year also had a knock-on effect. Military intervention to secure the Suez Canal caused an Egyptian boycott, swiftly backed by Iraq and Lebanon, which withdrew after demanding that nations "guilty of cowardly aggression against Egypt" (meaning Israel, Britain and France) should be expelled.

And although East and West Germany competed as one

37

team, at the other end of the globe China withdrew entirely in opposition to Taiwan being allowed to compete under the label 'Republic of China'.

Thus politics overshadowed sport, as it would often continue to do through the second half of the twentieth century. In 1956, with nations locked in the struggles of the Cold War, there were strong indications that the entire Games of the XVI Olympiad would have to be cancelled on the assumption that the rules disallowed warring nations to take part. But Avery Brundage, president of the International Olympic Committee, announced: "We will not let any country use the Olympics for political purposes."

The situation was most fraught for the Hungarian competitors, most of whom had been en route to Australia when the uprising in their homeland began and in training when the USSR sent in tanks to crush resistance. Fearing for their families, the Hungarians felt forced to continue but wept as they were greeted by Australian well-wishers and sang their national anthem under flags draped in black crepe.

In such volatile conditions an explosion of national feeling seemed inevitable – and happened in the most extraordinary circumstances. When Hungary met the USSR in the water polo semi-final, the match degenerated into a brawl, both above and below the surface. The referee was obliged to end the match with the Hungarians leading 4-0.

At the end of the Games more than half of the Hungarian team refused to travel back to Budapest, staying in Australia to seek political asylum. One who did return, however, was middleweight boxer Laszlo Papp, a southpaw who became the first boxer to win gold medals over three successive Olympiads, in 1948, 1952 and 1956, a feat since equalled but not surpassed.

Papp had beaten Britain's John Wright to win the middleweight title in the 1948 London Games and had beaten South Africa's Theunis van Schalkwyk to win the new light-middleweight title in Helsinki in 1952. His third Olympic gold, again at light-middleweight, came with a win over José Torres of the USA.

Melbourne did witness several other extraordinary scenes. After the Duke of Edinburgh opened the Games at Melbourne Cricket Ground, where a new track had been laid, the weather was so hot that several athletes fainted.

The Olympic flame was lit by nineteen-year-old Ron Clarke, the junior world mile record holder who was later to become one of history's greatest ever distance runners. He never enjoyed supreme luck in the

1956: MELBOURNE

Olympic arena, however, and is generally regarded as being the best runner never to have won a gold medal.

Soviet runner Vladimir Kuts was the star of the track, with record-breaking victories at 5,000 and 10,000 metres. In the latter, run on the first day, Kuts launched himself at an astonishing pace and only Britain's Gordon Pirie, who had recently been rivalling him in world records, could keep up with him. The two were 100 metres ahead of the field when, at 8,000 metres, the Briton overtook Kuts – only for the tough Ukranian marine to find the energy for one final sprint to victory.

Five days later Kuts was again challenged by Pirie, along with fellow countrymen Derek Ibbotson and Chris Chataway, in the 5,000 metres. Chataway had previously held the world record, as did Pirie at the time, and Ibbotson was to beat the mile world record the following year. Yet, again it was Kuts's day on the Australian track – justifying the description of him by another running legend, Roger Bannister, as "nature's attempt at an engine in boots".

His victories also seemed to justify the severe training regime that the Soviet coaches imposed on him. Before the 10,000 metres event, he had completed twenty-five fast quarter-miles with only thirty seconds of jogging between each. Such techniques eventually took their toll and the Soviet sporting hero died after a series of heart attacks in 1975, at the age of only forty-eight.

Among other memorable Melbourne track events, the 1,500 metres provided a rare but popular cause for Irish celebrations when Ron Delany, who had twice lost to Britain's Brian Hewson, sprinted to the tape to win his country's first gold medal since 1932.

America's Bobby-Joe Morrow and Australia's Elizabeth 'Betty' Cuthbert each won three gold medals in the sprint, including the relay. To her home crowd in Melbourne, eighteen-year-old Cuthbert became the heroine of the Games by capturing the 100 metres and 200 metres and helping the Australian sprint relay squad set two world records. A colleague of Cuthbert's in the relay was Shirley de la Hunty (nee Strickland), who ended her Olympic career with a total of seven medals, three gold, one silver and three bronze – a record that has never been beaten.

There was a controversial finish to the 3,000 metres steeplechase in which Britain's Chris Brasher crossed the line first but was disqualified for a supposed foul on Norway's Ernst Larsen. Although team-mate John Disley, a bronze medallist in 1952, was more fancied, Brasher had stormed to victory with a spectacular last lap in which he squeezed through a gap left by the two leaders to win in an Olympic record time.

Brasher was initially disqualified for pushing his way through and the race was awarded to the second man home, Hungary's Sandor Rozsnyoi. But, sportingly, all competitors involved spoke up for Brasher and his appeal was upheld, giving Britain its first athletics gold medal since 1936. Successfully reinstated, Brasher then almost missed the medal ceremony because he lingered in a local hotel celebrating with the British press corps. Brasher remained in the limelight long afterwards through an illustrious career in journalism and business, and founded the London Marathon in 1981.

A further cause of controversy and confusion at the Games of the XVI Olympiad was that, for the first and only time in Olympic history, the Summer Games were staged in two countries. Australia's stiff quarantine laws kept foreign horses out and the equestrian events were staged in Stockholm, even though this was contrary to the Olympic Charter. Riders criticised the state of the cross-country course, claiming it was too dangerous. And the final tally of medals, whereby Sweden won three of the six titles, prompted allegations of biased judging.

Happier highlights of the Games were Ukrainian gymnast Viktor Chukarin's five medals, including three gold, raising his career total to eleven medals, seven of them gold.

The USA basketball team put on the most dominant performance in Olympic history, scoring more than twice as much as their opponents and winning each of their games by at least thirty points.

Among the most popular results in Australia was the marathon winner Alain Mimoun. The Frenchman had thrice followed the legendary Emil Zatopek home in Olympic events. The Czech runner confined himself to the marathon for his Olympian farewell and finished sixth. Mimoun patiently waited for Zatopek at the finish and the two friends took the crowd's rapturous applause together.

While some of the clashes in Australia showed that not every element of the Melbourne Games could be classed as 'friendly', a new tradition was begun there in 1956 that attempted to put politics aside for the sake of sport. Prior to 1956, athletes in the closing ceremony had marched around the stadium nation by nation. In Melbourne, however, all the competitors entered *en masse* as a symbol of global unity.

MEDALS TABLE
MELBOURNE 1956 – GAMES OF THE XVI OLYMPIAD
SUMMER OLYMPIC GAMES

Nation	Gold	Silver	Bronze	Total
Soviet Union	37	29	32	98
United States	32	25	17	74
Australia	13	8	14	35
Hungary	9	10	7	26
Italy	8	8	9	25
Sweden	8	5	6	19
Germany	6	13	7	26
Great Britain	6	7	11	24
Romania	5	3	5	13
Japan	4	10	5	19
France	4	4	6	14
Turkey	3	2	2	7
Finland	3	1	11	15
Iran	2	2	1	5
Canada	2	1	3	6
New Zealand	2	0	0	2
Poland	1	4	4	9
Czechoslovakia	1	4	1	6
Bulgaria	1	3	1	5
Denmark	1	2	1	4
Ireland	1	1	3	5
Norway	1	0	2	3
Mexico	1	0	1	2
Brazil	1	0	0	1
India	1	0	0	1
Yugoslavia	0	3	0	3
Chile	0	2	2	4
Belgium	0	2	0	2
Argentina	0	1	1	2
South Korea	0	1	1	2
Iceland	0	1	0	1
Pakistan	0	1	0	1

Nation	Gold	Silver	Bronze	Total
South Africa	0	0	4	4
Austria	0	0	2	2
Bahamas	0	0	1	1
Greece	0	0	1	1
Switzerland	0	0	1	1
Uruguay	0	0	1	1

SPORTS - MELBOURNE 1956

Events: 145 in 19 sports – Athletics | Basketball | Boxing | Canoeing |Cycling | Diving | Equestrian | Fencing | Football (soccer) | Gymnastics | Hockey | Modern pentathlon | Rowing | Sailing | Shooting | Swimming | Water polo | Weightlifting | Wrestling.

CHAPTER 5

1960: Rome

25 August – 11 September

Games of the XVII Olympiad

Countries participating: 83

Athletes participating:
5,338 (4,727 men, 611 women)

Events: 150 in 19 sports

 Rome had endured a long wait for its chance to host the Olympic Games. Back in 1904, Coubertin himself had expressed his fervent wish to have the Olympics hosted there, saying: "I desired Rome only because I wanted Olympism, after its return from the excursion to utilitarian America, to don once again the sumptuous toga, woven of art and philosophy, in which I had always wanted to clothe her."

The city had been due to host the Games of 1908 but the eruption of Mount Vesuvius in April 1906 forced the Italian government to switch its funding away from sport into a massive rescue operation. Instead, London took the Games of the IV Olympiad.

Indeed it had been an even longer wait for Rome's opportunity to resurrect the Games. The ancient Olympics had been abolished by Roman Emperor Theodosius in AD 393 and were not revived until 1896. But the gap of over 1,500 years was bridged in warm and colourful style by the Italians in 1960.

The Games of the XVII Olympiad, held from 25 August to

11 September, was a fitting merger of ancient and modern. The 5,348 athletes from 83 countries, having been welcomed to 'the Eternal City' by the Pope, competed in venues old and new. Gymnastics took place in the Terme di Caracalla, the wrestling in the Basilica di Massenzio and the marathon began at Capitol Hill and finished on the Appian Way, near the Arch of Constantine. Newer sites included the marble stadia built by wartime dictator Mussolini in forlorn anticipation of hosting the event in 1944. There were also magnificent new arenas, notably the Velodrome for cycling and the Sports Palace for boxing.

Canoeing took place outside Rome on Lake Albano near the summer residence of the Pope, who was seen watching the action. Other waterborne events were held to the south under the shadow of Mount Vesuvius, where yachtsmen competed in the Bay of Naples. There Crown Prince Constantine, heir to the Greek throne, became a rare royal gold medalist when he won in the Dragon class.

There were other notable 'firsts' – and one significant 'last' – in 1960. South Africa, which had always insisted on fielding an all-white team, appeared for the last time under its apartheid regime. It would not return to the arena until 1992, following transition to majority rule.

One modest hero of the Games, Abebe Bikila of Ethiopia, became the first black African to win an Olympic gold medal. Bikila's triumphant Italian marathon was a very personal victory as members of his family had been killed during Mussolini's invasion of his country in the Thirties. The marathon, staged by moonlight, was run barefoot by Bikila in 2 hours 15 minutes 17 seconds, presaging an influx of African runners into world distance events and emphasising the spread of medals with each passing Games. In Rome a record forty-four countries shared the medals.

Another competitor who rocketed to global recognition was eighteen-year-old Cassius Clay, who won the light heavyweight title and went on to dominate heavyweight boxing in the Sixties and Seventies. Under his new name Muhammad Ali he became probably the best known sportsman in the history of the world.

A speedy hero of the Games was Australia's Herb Elliott, who captured the 1,500 metres crown with one of the finest displays of middle-distance running ever witnessed, breaking his own world record to win by almost three seconds, at 3 minutes 35.6 seconds.

An American's achievement justifiably celebrated in 1960 was Wilma Rudolph whose life story was later made into a movie 'Wilma'. One of

1960: ROME

twenty-two children, and a teen mother herself, she had suffered double pneumonia, scarlet fever and polio, leaving her left leg withered and paralysed. Yet she won the rapture of the Rome crowds with her three gold medals: the women's 100 and 200 metres and the 400-metre relay.

Jeff Farrell of the United States also overcame last-minute adversity when he won two gold medals in swimming after undergoing an emergency appendectomy six days before the Olympic Trials.

A tragic first for the Games was the death of Danish cyclist Knut Jensen, who collapsed during the road race. It was the second time an athlete had died in competition, the first being Portuguese marathon runner Francisco Lazaro in Stockholm in 1912. But Jensen was the first athlete to die in the Games as a result of performance-enhancing drugs.

As well as drugs, another curse, and one that continued to blight the Games over ensuing decades, was politics. The People's Republic of China chose to boycott the Olympics because of the inclusion of Taiwan in the Games. Divided Germany, however, was pressed by the International Olympic Committee to put politics aside for a brief period, and both East and West competed together.

The principal controversy during the events themselves arose over a ruling in the 100 metre freestyle swim. John Devitt of Australia and Lance Larson of the United States had finished the race virtually neck and neck. Sports journalists, the audience and the swimmers themselves believed the American had won but the three judges chose Devitt. Even though the official times showed a faster time for Larson than for Devitt, the ruling held but the ensuing row led to the introduction of full electronic timing for future Games.

One final innovation... the 1960 Games were the first Olympics to be fully covered by television. They were broadcast live in eighteen European countries and, with only a few hours delay, to the United States, Canada and Japan.

Those viewers were the first to hear the rousing Olympic Anthem, adopted two years earlier by the IOC as the official theme for the Games. The anthem had originally been composed by Spiros Samaras for the 1896 Athens venue – but it was not until Rome was host in 1960 that it was first played at an Olympic Games.

The Rome Games were noted for the friendly nature of competing countries and individual athletes. Soviet officials displayed good sportsmanship and unprecedented friendliness, perhaps with good reason because they proved that the United States could be surpassed in overall performance. The Americans, though still leading in track and field, no longer dominated the honours as more nations put forward medal-winning candidates.

At the close of the Games, as the light dimmed, the 100,000 crowd in the magnificent Stadio Olympico illuminated the euphoric scene by lighting torches from furled newspapers. Meanwhile, an artillery battery blasted away and fireworks lit the sky. The understandable enthusiasm resulted in cars, gardens and tinder-dry woods going up in smoke.

Despite such mishaps the end result of the Rome Olympics was that Italy, a country that craved approbation fifteen years after the end of World War II and its destructive flirtation with fascist militarism, became a nation universally admired for hosting a colourful, joyful and highly successful XVII Olympiad.

1960: ROME

MEDALS TABLE
ROME 1960 – GAMES OF THE XVII OLYMPIAD
SUMMER OLYMPIC GAMES

Nation	Gold	Silver	Bronze	Total
Soviet Union	43	29	31	103
United States	34	21	16	71
Italy	13	10	13	36
Germany	12	19	11	42
Australia	8	8	6	22
Turkey	7	2	0	9
Hungary	6	8	7	21
Japan	4	7	7	18
Poland	4	6	11	21
Czechoslovakia	3	2	3	8
Romania	3	1	6	10
Great Britain	2	6	12	20
Denmark	2	3	1	6
New Zealand	2	0	1	3
Bulgaria	1	3	3	7
Sweden	1	2	3	6
Finland	1	1	3	5
Austria	1	1	0	2
Yugoslavia	1	1	0	2
Pakistan	1	0	1	2
Ethiopia	1	0	0	1
Greece	1	0	0	1
Norway	1	0	0	1
Switzerland	0	3	3	6
France	0	2	3	5
Belgium	0	2	2	4
Iran	0	1	3	4
Netherlands	0	1	2	3
South Africa	0	1	2	3
Argentina	0	1	1	2
United Arab Republic	0	1	1	2
Canada	0	1	0	1

Nation	Gold	Silver	Bronze	Total
Republic of China	0	1	0	1
Ghana	0	1	0	1
India	0	1	0	1
Morocco	0	1	0	1
Portugal	0	1	0	1
Singapore	0	1	0	1
Brazil	0	0	2	2
British West Indies	0	0	2	2
Iraq	0	0	1	1
Mexico	0	0	1	1
Spain	0	0	1	1
Venezuela	0	0	1	1

SPORTS - ROME 1960

Events: 150 in 19 sports – Athletics | Basketball | Boxing | Canoeing | Cycling | Diving | Equestrian | Fencing | Football (soccer) | Gymnastics | Hockey | Modern pentathlon | Rowing | Sailing | Shooting | Swimming | Water polo | Weightlifting | Wrestling.

CHAPTER 6

1964: Tokyo

10 October – 24 October

Games of the XVIII Olympiad

Countries participating: 93

Athletes participating:
5,151 (4,473 men, 678 women)

Events: 163 in 21 sports

 Ten thousand pigeons of peace were released to mark the opening of the Tokyo Olympic Games on 10 October 1964. But despite Japan's best efforts towards international reconciliation, memories of past conflict still haunted the XVIII Olympics.

The last lap by torchbearers to light the Olympic flame was run by nineteen-year-old Yoshinoro Saki, born near Hiroshima on the day the atomic bomb incinerated the city in 1945. The official opening was performed by Emperor Hirohito, amidst bitter protests from former prisoners of war about his country's brutal regime only two decades before.

The decision to award the Games to Tokyo had in itself been an act of reconciliation towards Japan. In return, and determined to demonstrate the changes it had made since the end of World War II, the nation spent a staggering £2 billion on building new stadia and improving the city's infrastructure.

Visitors and media were impressed by the hospitality offered, the latter labelling it the 'Happy Games'. And happiness was a much needed global commodity in 1964

following such recent world events as the building of the Berlin Wall, China's first nuclear test, the assassination of President Kennedy and the US embroilment in Vietnam. So these Games provided a welcome relief to the multi-millions now able to watch them through the advance of technology.

Since the Rome Games four years earlier, an orbital network of global communications had been formed and, with satellites like Telstar in operation, the Olympic Games were seen live for the first time in the sitting rooms of the world. Another innovation that heralded this new age for the Games was the computerisation of the events, with scoring and timekeeping all recorded electronically.

Sixteen nations made their first appearance in Tokyo: Algeria, Cameroon, Chad, Congo, Ivory Coast, Domnican Republic, Libya, Madagascar, Malaysia, Mali, Mongolia, Nepal, Niger, Senegal and Tanganyika – plus Northern Rhodesia, which achieved full independence as Zambia on the same day as the closing ceremony. South Africa, however, was unwelcome because of its apartheid policies and it was to be almost thirty years before its athletes were to reappear on the Olympic arena.

Once the Games got underway, another newcomer was introduced. At the behest of the host nation, judo was added to the events. The Japanese firmly believed they were guaranteed every gold medal in this sport but they were massively shocked when Dutchman Anton Geesink won the open gold. The 6ft 6ins giant said: "Everyone in Japan was desperate for one of their players to win and the arena fell silent when I did. Then the crowd rose to applaud me. They appreciated what I had achieved."

Another unexpected win – indeed, one of the biggest upsets in Olympic history – came when America's Billy Mills sprinted to victory in the 10,000 metres in a Games record of 28 minutes 28.4 seconds. It was a personal best by an incredible forty-six seconds.

Mills, a part-Sioux native American and a US Marine officer, said immediately afterwards: "I'm flabbergasted. I suppose I was the only person who thought I had a chance." Japanese officials were also dumbfounded. As they surrounded the unexpected winner, one of them asked him: "Who are you?"

Another popular hero of the track was New Zealand's Peter Snell, who achieved an amazing double, having decided to attempt both the 800 metres and the 1,500 metres – which meant racing six times. Having previously set world records from 800 metres to the mile, he retained the 800 metres and then added the 1,500 metres gold medal, despite never having raced the distance before arriving in Japan. His dual-champion performance made him the only man to achieve this feat since 1920.

The sprint titles, all of which had eluded the Americans in 1960, returned to the United States in 1964. And it was the seemingly ungainly Bob Hayes who produced what some track experts still believe to be the greatest sprint performance in history. In a wind-assisted semi-final, he recorded what would have been a world record of 9.9 seconds. In the final he equalled the world record of 10 seconds. He also anchored the US to gold in the 4 x 100 metres with a phenomenal final leg.

Britain also enjoyed one of its most successful games thanks to its women. Mary Rand became the first British woman to strike gold when she took the long jump. Then her team-mate Ann Packer won the 800 metres.

Betty Cuthbert, the golden girl of Australian athletics, had triumphed in Melbourne but had missed out on the 1960 Games because of a hamstring injury. After a brief retirement she returned to the track in 1964 to compete in the 400 metres, a new event for women, and she was its first winner. Her total of four gold medal in four attempts equalled the 1948 record of Fanny Blankers-Koen.

However, the most successful athlete of the Games was the nineteen-year-old Soviet-Ukranian gymnast Larissa Latynina. Almost single-handedly responsible for establishing the Soviet Union as the dominant force in gymnastics, she followed successes in Melbourne and Rome by winning two golds, two silvers and two bronzes in Tokyo.

Her records still stand: as the only female athlete to win nine Olympic golds, the most individual medals (fourteen outside of team events) and eighteen medals in total, more than any other competitor in any sport in Olympic history. She is also the only woman who has won an individual event (floor exercise) in three Olympics (1956, 1960, and 1964).

At the other end of the weight spectrum Joe Frazier – the mighty American who was to go on to produce some fantastic clashes with Muhammad Ali – unexpectedly won the heavyweight gold medal.

Frazier, who had trained as an amateur by punching dead carcasses while working as a Philadelphia meat packer, had been beaten in Olympic trials by his countryman Buster Mathis, a fighter with a far better amateur record. However, Mathis broke his thumb while training and

'Smokin' Joe Frazier had the advantage. Then, in the Olympic semi-finals, Frazier broke his own thumb. He had the thumb taped, fought like fury in the finals with his one good hand and won gold.

One female contestant at the Tokyo Games was almost as fiery as 'Smokin' Joe. Australia's Dawn Fraser won her third consecutive 100 metres freestyle title, becoming the only swimmer to win three consecutive Olympic titles in the same event. She added a relay silver to take her total haul to eight medals – four golds and four silvers between 1956 and 1964 – a record for a female swimmer. Often referred to as 'the greatest female swimmer of all time', she set twenty-seven individual world records, perhaps the most memorable by becoming the first woman to swim the 100 metre distance in under a minute.

However, Dawn's talent was in many ways overshadowed by her equally lively style away from the water. Though loved by Australian sports fans she was in constant battles with officialdom. In Rome four years earlier she had refused to swim in a medley relay and was sent to Coventry by her team-mates. But in 1964 she got into deeper water.

Dawn led a night raid on the Emperor's Palace to steal a souvenir Japanese flag from atop a flagpole. She was arrested but charges were dropped and the Emperor gave her a flag as a gift. The Aussie public rejoiced at her stunt but the nation's Olympic officials were so embarrassed they forced her to make a public apology. The Australian Swimming Union was even more unforgiving, imposing a ten-year suspension, later lifted after four years. It effectively marked the end of Fraser's career at the tender age of twenty-seven and deprived her of the chance of what might have been a record-shattering fourth consecutive 100 metre gold.

Another consecutive winner was Ethiopia's Abebe Bikila, the modest barefoot marathon hero of the Rome Games. He was not expected to compete in Tokyo, having collapsed with acute appendicitis only weeks before, but he started jogging in the grounds of the Addis Ababa hospital within days of his operation. When he arrived in Japan it was assumed he would be a spectator but he entered the marathon, this time wearing Puma shoes.

As in Rome, Bikila reserved his energies until, after 15 kilometres, he increased his seemingly effortless pace. He entered the Olympic stadium alone to the cheers of 70,000 spectators, leaving Britain's Basil Heatley and Japan's Kokichi Tsuburaya trailing second and third. While waiting for them to finish the inexhaustible Ethiopian astonished the crowd by occupying himself with a routine of stretching exercises. He later said, without the hint of boastfulness, that he could have run another ten kilometres. Bikila was the first athlete in history to win the Olympic marathon twice.

There was a sad postscript to the event, however. Kokichi Tsuburaya, who had been overtaken by Basil Heatley only in the last 100 metres, believed he had let down his country by winning only a bronze. Subsequently suffering from depression, as well as lumbago, he committed suicide by cutting his own throat in 1968, at the age of 28. In his suicide note, he apologized for having failed his country and wrote: "I am too tired to run any more."

MEDALS TABLE
TOKYO 1964 – GAMES OF THE XVIII OLYMPIAD
SUMMER OLYMPIC GAMES

Nation	Gold	Silver	Bronze	Total
United States	36	26	28	90
Soviet Union	30	31	35	96
Japan	16	5	8	29
Germany	10	22	18	50
Italy	10	10	7	27
Hungary	10	7	5	22
Poland	7	6	10	23
Australia	6	2	10	18
Czechoslovakia	5	6	3	14
Great Britain	4	12	2	18
Bulgaria	3	5	2	10
Finland	3	0	2	5
New Zealand	3	0	2	5
Romania	2	4	6	12
Netherlands	2	4	4	10
Turkey	2	3	1	6
Sweden	2	2	4	8
Denmark	2	1	3	6
Yugoslavia	2	1	2	5
Belgium	2	0	1	3
France	1	8	6	15
Canada	1	2	1	4
Switzerland	1	2	1	4
Bahamas	1	0	0	1
Ethiopia	1	0	0	1
India	1	0	0	1
South Korea	0	2	1	3
Trinidad and Tobago	0	1	2	3
Tunisia	0	1	1	2
Argentina	0	1	0	1
Cuba	0	1	0	1
Pakistan	0	1	0	1
Philippines	0	1	0	1

1964: TOKYO

Nation	Gold	Silver	Bronze	Total
Iran	0	0	2	2
Brazil	0	0	1	1
Ghana	0	0	1	1
Ireland	0	0	1	1
Kenya	0	0	1	1
Mexico	0	0	1	1
Nigeria	0	0	1	1
Uruguay	0	0	1	1

SPORTS - TOKYO 1964

Events: 163 in 21 sports – Athletics | Basketball | Boxing | Canoeing | Cycling | Diving | Equestrian | Fencing | Football (soccer) | Gymnastics | Hockey | Judo | Modern pentathlon | Rowing | Sailing | Shooting | Swimming | Volleyball | Water polo | Weightlifting | Wrestling.

CHAPTER 7

1968: Mexico City

12 October – 27 October

Games of the XIX Olympiad

Countries participating: 112

Athletes participating:
5,516 (4,735 men, 781 women)

Events: 172 in 22 sports

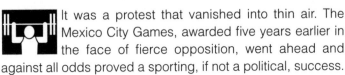 It was a protest that vanished into thin air. The Mexico City Games, awarded five years earlier in the face of fierce opposition, went ahead and against all odds proved a sporting, if not a political, success.

The main controversy was a medical one: the thin air of Mexico City, nearly 2,240 metres above sea level. No other Summer Olympics have been held at a location remotely as high and it was feared that the altitude might be harmful – and even fatal in the distance events.

But as the Games of the XIX Olympiad got underway, the high altitude and the thin air seemed to pump more oxygen into the athlete's muscles. They were factors credited with contributing to many record-setting times in the shorter track events and with extra-spectacular leaps in the high jump, long jump, triple jump and pole vault.

One man who hit the heights, literally, was America's Bob Beamon. In the long jump he leapt 8.90 metres, an incredible 55 centimetres over the previous world record – and one that would stand for twenty-three years until it was broken by America's Mike Powell in 1991. In the more familiar feet and inches of the time, Beamon's leap was 29 feet, 2$\frac{1}{2}$ inches, almost two feet beyond the previous world mark. Boosted by the maximum permitted wind aid, he hit the sand so powerfully with his first jump that he bounced back up and landed outside the pit.

An equally astonishing performance came from sixteen-year-old American Dick Fosbury, who revolutionised the high jump by inventing a new style of clearing the bar that became known as the 'Fosbury Flop'. Until he came along most jumpers went over the bar forwards, using the straddle technique or sideways with the western roll. Fosbury developed a style which involved running at the bar on a curved approach and turning to jump backwards while arching the back and bringing the lap up high. He won the gold medal in Mexico City by clearing 2.24 metres. He never jumped so high again.

In the triple jump the previous world record was improved five times by three different athletes.

America's sixteen-year-old Debbie Meyer became the first swimmer to win three individual gold medals, in the 200, 400 and 800 metre freestyle events. Her countryman Charles Hickcox won three gold medals – in both the 200 and 400 individual medleys (setting an Olympic record in the 200) and with the US 400 medley relay team – plus a silver in the 100 backstroke. It was the peak of Hickcox's career, for within just sixteen months the swimmer set eight world records.

Other multi-victories were notched up in Mexico City. American discus thrower Al Oerta won his fourth consecutive gold medal to become only the second athlete to achieve this feat in an individual event. Czechoslovakia's Vera Caslavska proved herself the world's greatest gymnast. Having taken three golds and a silver at Tokyo four years earlier, she won four gold medals and two silver medals at Mexico City.

Records were also overturned on the track where Americans Jim Hines and Lee Evans set long-standing world firsts in the 100 metres and 400 metres. Evans won the 400 in a record 43.86 seconds. It took a further twenty years before anyone else managed to crack 44 seconds.

The XIX Games were also notable for the emergence of African distance runners. Kip Keino of Kenya almost failed to make the 1,500 metres after getting caught in one of Mexico City's notorious traffic jams.

But he jogged the last mile to the stadium – and thereby put Kenya on course to become a future world force in middle and long-distance running.

Keino, whose loping stride, toothy smile and unpredictable tactics made him a crowd-pleaser, had already overcome one disappointment when stomach cramps struck him two laps short of finishing the 10,000 metres final. Four days later he finished second in the 5,000 metres. Then came the 1,500 in which he upset all the odds by front-running his way to a sensational victory over the American world record holder and favourite, Jim Ryun. Four years later Keino went on to win a further gold in the 3,000 metres steeplechase and a silver in the 1,500 metres.

It was America's black athletes, however, for whom the Mexican Games will be remembered – and not always for their sporting prowess. They won seven of the twelve US men's track and field gold medals, setting five world records, while black American women won three golds and set two world records.

The most memorable victor was Tommie Smith, who set a world record of 19.83 seconds in the 200 metres. But that was because his dash was overshadowed by the protest he and his team-mate, bronze medallist John Carlos, staged as they awaited the presentation of their medals.

The pair mounted the podium wearing civil rights badges and with bare feet as a reminder of black poverty in the United States. When 'The Star-Spangled Banner' was played, they bowed their heads and each one raised a black-gloved hand in the Black Power salute. It was a gesture that stunned the world and particularly shocked middle-America.

The pair were unrepentant. "I did it because I was afraid to do it, understand?" explained Smith. "I knew what I was going to do might get me killed. But it had to be done. I felt the necessity for change."

John Carlos said: "We got letters saying 'You set us back a hundred years' and others saying, 'You freed us'. The verdict is still out."

The US Olympic Committee disapproved but was unwilling to make martyrs of Smith and Carlos. But IOC chief Avery Brundage threatened to expel the entire US team if the pair remained unpunished on the grounds that abuse of the ban on political demonstration would cause total degeneration of the Games. Two days later Smith and Carlos were expelled from the US team and ordered home.

The expulsion served only to rally their team-mates behind them. Bob Beamon wore black socks to receive his gold medal for his world record in the long jump. Lee Evans, Larry James and Ron Freeman, the gold, silver and bronze medallists in the 400 metres, donned the berets of the militant Black Panthers on the podium. Subsequently, Muhammad Ali described the Smith-Carlos protest as "the single most courageous act of this century" and Wimbledon champion Arthur Ashe said it was "an inspiration to a generation".

Somewhat overshadowed in all of this was the fact that Peter Norman of Australia, who had run second in the 200 metres, finishing between Smith and Carlos, had also worn an American civil rights badge as support for them on the podium. As punishment, Norman was left off the Australian 1972 Olympic team.

The demonstrations tainted what was generally acknowledged to have been the greatest track meet in history, as records galore tumbled. But it might never have happened.

Before the facilities for the XIX Olympics were even built, Mexico City had been rocked by violent protests at the vast cost of hosting the Games in a relatively impoverished country. Student demonstrations that centred on the Plaza de las Tres Culturas (Square of the Three Cultures) culminated in a confrontation between 10,000 protesters and the Mexican army in which 260 people were killed and another 1,200 were injured.

The Games went ahead but not before international politics had caused further dissent. For the first time, athletes from East and West Germany were members of separate teams, after having been compelled to compete in an all-German team since 1956. But one nation was entirely banned. Black African countries, backed by black members of the American team, threatened a boycott if South Africa was admitted and, after long deliberation, the IOC gave in.

The protest that remained most memorable, however, involved neither foreign diplomacy nor guns and riots... just two raised fists.

MEDALS TABLE
MEXICO CITY 1968 – GAMES OF THE XIX OLYMPIAD
SUMMER OLYMPIC GAMES

Nation	Gold	Silver	Bronze	Total
United States	45	28	34	107
Soviet Union	29	32	30	91
Japan	11	7	7	25
Hungary	10	10	12	32
East Germany	9	9	7	25
France	7	3	5	15
Czechoslovakia	7	2	4	13
West Germany	5	11	10	26
Australia	5	7	5	17
Great Britain	5	5	3	13
Poland	5	2	11	18
Romania	4	6	5	15
Italy	3	4	9	16
Kenya	3	4	2	9
Mexico	3	3	3	9
Yugoslavia	3	3	2	8
Netherlands	3	3	1	7
Bulgaria	2	4	3	9
Iran	2	1	2	5
Sweden	2	1	1	4
Turkey	2	0	0	2
Denmark	1	4	3	8
Canada	1	3	1	5
Finland	1	2	1	4
Ethiopia	1	1	0	2
Norway	1	1	0	2
New Zealand	1	0	2	3
Tunisia	1	0	1	2
Pakistan	1	0	0	1
Venezuela	1	0	0	1
Cuba	0	4	0	4
Austria	0	2	2	4
Switzerland	0	1	4	5

Nation	Gold	Silver	Bronze	Total
Mongolia	0	1	3	4
Brazil	0	1	2	3
Belgium	0	1	1	2
South Korea	0	1	1	2
Uganda	0	1	1	2
Cameroon	0	1	0	1
Jamaica	0	1	0	1
Argentina	0	0	2	2
Greece	0	0	1	1
India	0	0	1	1
Republic of China	0	0	1	1

SPORTS – MEXICO CITY 1968

Events: 172 in 22 sports – Athletics | Basketball | Basque Pelota | Boxing | Canoeing | Cycling | Diving | Equestrian | Fencing | Football (soccer) | Hockey | Gymnastics | Modern pentathlon | Rowing | Sailing | Shooting | Swimming | Tennis | Volleyball | Water polo | Weightlifting | Wrestling.

CHAPTER 8

1972: Munich

26 August – 10 September

Games of the XX Olympiad

Countries participating: 121

Athletes participating:
7,134 (6,075 men, 1,059 women)

Events: 195 in 25 sports

These were the Games that changed international sport forever. On the morning of 5 September, eight members of the Palestinian terrorist group Black September scaled the wire fence surrounding the Olympic Village and burst into the Israeli team quarters.

The first person to come face to face with the raiders was a wrestling coach who answered a knock on the door at 4.55am, found himself staring into the barrel of a gun and slammed it shut again. Bravely using his body as a barricade, he shouted a warning, which was quickly silenced when a burst of gunfire through the door killed him. In another room, a weightlifter who tried to hold back the gunmen with just a knife was also shot dead.

The events of the next few hours were played out in all their grim horror to television viewers around the world.

The gunmen, a breakaway group of the Palestine Liberation Organisation, had invaded the Olympic village to demand the release of 200 Arab prisoners languishing in Israeli jails. After the first two murders they took hostage nine other Israeli team members, who failed to flee in time, and roped them together on their beds, threatening to kill them too if their demands were not met.

A nail-biting twenty-hour stalemate followed as, with the Olympic village ringed by armour, the German foreign ministry sought an Arab nation to act as mediator to negotiate the freeing of the hostages. The Israeli government, however, was unbending; it rejected the prisoner releases and authorised West Germany to take all drastic measures necessary to free their athletes.

While the eyes of the world were focussed on the drama, the competition events of the XX Olympiad went ahead as scheduled. The surreal situation continued until mid-afternoon when the IOC halted the Games, unable to say whether they would ever resume.

As darkness fell the German authorities allowed the terrorists to take their blindfolded hostages by bus and by two helicopters the fifteen miles to a military airbase where a Lufthansa passenger jet awaited, supposedly to fly them to Cairo. Then to the world's horror, the police assault intended to stop them went tragically wrong.

Sharpshooters were poised to pick off the guerrillas but opened fire too soon. As the Arabs left one of the helicopters, shots rang out and one of the captors tossed a grenade into the second helicopter, in which the hostages were still trapped. It exploded in a fireball.

After the one-hour gunfight, all nine hostages were dead: wrestlers, weightlifters, a track and field coach, a rifle team coach and a fencing coach. Also killed were a German policeman and five of the terrorists. Three terrorists were captured.

A further victim of this debacle was whatever remained of the innocence of the Olympic Games. The West German authorities were accused of bungling the rescue and causing what many considered an unnecessary bloodbath. IOC president Avery Brundage was also criticised for his call to "let the Games go on".

And, of course, there were overriding questions about the lax security at the Olympic sites. The German authorities, recalling the shame of the 1936 Munich Games, had been determined to erase any hint of militarism. Police had been issued with casual sporting uniforms. Curfews were easily broken, so that athletes constantly slipped in and out of the Olympic village. This had been the reason why a group of casually dressed men had been able to scale a fence in the middle of the night and take from their innocent looking sports bags an armoury of Kalashnikovs.

The instant effect of the attack was to usher in an era of ever-tighter security around athletes and fans. Reinforcements were drafted in to

Dating from about 470BC, a Greek vase showing runners in the Olympic Games.

Seated left is Baron Pierre de Coubertin, along with other members of the organising committee of the first modern Games in Athens in 1896.

The Greek royal family lead the parade in 1896 at the start of the first modern Games.

Depiction of Spyridon Louis finishing the 1896 marathon, accompanied on the last lap by Prince Georg of Greece.

Spyridon Louis, the Greek shepherd who won the 1896 marathon.

London 1908... March past of the opening ceremony of the IV Olympiad at the White City Stadium in the presence of King Edward VII.

68

The start of the 100 metres final at the London Olympics of 1908, which was won by Reggie Walker of South Africa (in the far lane).

Celebrations after Henry Taylor of Great Britain won the freestyle relay.

Dorando Pietri running through the streets of London in the marathon of 1908 before his lead and victory were sadly taken away from him.

Before being disqualified, Dorando Pietri reaches the finishing line of the marathon with concerned officials close at hand.

XIVTH OLYMPIAD
LONDON 1948

OPENING CEREMONY

EMPIRE STADIUM WEMBLEY
THURSDAY 29TH JULY
AT 2.30 PM

Official Programme Two Shillings

London 1948... The original programme, signed by some of the competing athletes.

The Olympic Torch is lit at Olympia before the start of the relay from Greece to Britain.

The Olympic Torch is carried across the River Thames on its journey to London. Windsor Castle is in the background

King George VI salutes the athletes as they arrive during the Opening Ceremony.

General scene of the opening ceremony at Wembley Stadium as the torch is borne in.

The final runner in the torch relay enters the stadium during the opening ceremony and stands in salute beneath the scoreboard on which is emblazoned the Olympic motto.

The flame is lit, with warm words from Games chairman Lord Burghley, himself a gold medal winner at the 1928 Olympics, who described it as "a warm flame of hope for a better understanding in the world which has burned so low".

Words on the scoreboard… "The important thing in the Olympic Games is not winning but taking part. The essential thing in life is not conquering but fighting well."

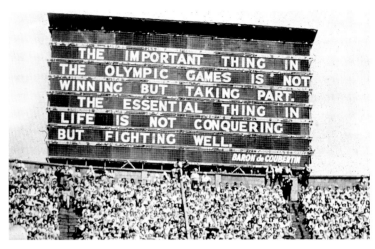

Throwing the discus… decathlon winner Bob Mathias of the United States, aged just seventeen.

Emil Zatopek of Czechoslovakia winning the 10,000 metres, three-quarters of a minute ahead of his nearest rival.

Gaston Rieff of Belgium after narrowly defeating Emil Zatopek in the 5,000 metres. A few days earlier Zatopek had lowered the 10,000 metres world record by 12 seconds.

Legendary heroine of the 1948 Olympics… Fanny Blankers-Koen receives her gold medal for the 200 metres. Silver went to Britain's Audrey Williamson and bronze to America's Audrey Patterson.

Unveiling of the Commemoration Tablets listing the 1948 Olympic champions.

Close-up of one of the pair of Commemoration Tablets, which is still housed at the new Wembley Stadium.

guard the Munich Games against further acts of terrorism that were still feared – the British team having received death threats from the IRA. Athletes attended a memorial service for their fellow Olympians in the main stadium, where Avery Brundage announced that the Games would go on after a 24-hour postponement.

And when the Games began again the events produced plenty of sporting heroes to lift the spirits at Munich. The enduring names included American swimmer Mark Spitz, Russian gymnast Olga Korbut and British pentathlete Mary Peters.

Spitz was undoubtedly the star of the show. The twenty-two-year-old had already won two relay golds, a silver and a bronze at the 1968 Games, and his ambition at Munich was to better the record of four golds at a single Games. He launched his attempt with a victory and world record in the 200 metres butterfly, followed by golds and world records in the 100 metres and 200 metres freestyle, 100 metres butterfly and three relays.

Mark Spitz left Germany with a record seven gold medals, the only sour note in the historic conquests being when he waved his shoes at the TV cameras and then had to convince the IOC that he had not been paid to do so. Nevertheless, after the Games the handsome all-American hero went on to become the first athlete to make a fortune out of corporate sponsorships.

Olga Korbutt also captivated the watching world in 1972 as, appearing in her first international event, she performed daring back flips on the uneven bars and balance beam. The 4 foot 11 inch, 85 pound, pigtailed seventeen-year-old from Belarus became the world's first gymnastics superstar.

Korbut, who stole the show from under the nose of the overall champion, Lyudmila Turischeva, was so isolated within the Soviet team quarters that she was blind to the international sensation she had caused until she was inundated with flowers, gifts and letters from all over the world. Her reward: three golds and a silver.

Another firm favourite in 1972 was Mary Peters, a secretary from Northern Ireland, then at the height of 'the Troubles'. She received a death threat during the Games but did not reveal the fact until years afterwards.

Bidding for the pentathlon the thirty-three-year-old, who had come fourth in Tokyo and ninth in Mexico City, knew that Munich was her last chance. She dedicated her efforts to her terrorist-ravaged home town of Belfast, saying beforehand: "The silver medal is useless to me. It has to be the gold or nothing, a gold medal for Belfast. Something good has to happen to our city."

She was as good as her word and produced two days of spell-binding performances. Peters notched up two personal bests on the first day, in the 100 metres hurdles and the high jump, to gain a ninety-seven-point lead over the West German favourite Heide Rosendahl. But the contest between the two went to the line when, on the second day, Peters knew she had to run a personal best in the 200 metres to beat her rival. The gap between Peters' 24.08 seconds and Rosendahl's 22.96 seconds was indeed narrow enough to gain her the gold – with a new world record total for the pentathlon of 4,801 points. Even the German fans at the stadium ended up rooting for Mary Peters and Rosendahl was the first to congratulate her.

In other memorable highlights another West German, Ulrike Meyfarth became the youngest Olympic high jump champion at the age of sixteen years 123 days. Using the Fosbury Flop technique, she won the high jump with a new world record of 1.92 metres.

Another heroine of Munich was Australian swimmer Shane Gould who, just short of her sixteenth birthday, won three gold medals plus a silver and a bronze. The golds were in the 200 metres individual medley and the 200 and 400 freestyle – setting a world record in each. The silver was for the 800 metres freestyle; the bronze for the 100 freestyle. It was the greatest performance by an Australian at a single Olympics, and when Gould retired, at just sixteen, she was the only person, male or female, to hold every world freestyle record from 100 metres to 1,500 metres simultaneously.

The most controversial sporting decision of the Olympics came when the US lost the gold-medal basketball game to the Soviet Union after being awarded three tries at the final field goal. In protest at this bizarre case of officiating, the American team failed to appear in the Olympiastadion for the awards ceremonies and continued to refuse their silver medals, which went into store in an IOC vault in Lausanne, Switzerland.

The fact that, as the Games proceeded, the world was again able to focus on pure sport rather than crude and bloody politics was evidence of the supremacy of the Olympic spirit. This was summed up most eloquently by American marathon winner Frank Shorter who said:

"We went through the stages humans go through in times of brutal stress – from denial to anger, to grief, to resolve. But we could not let this detract from our performance, because that's what they wanted. To surrender in Munich would be to surrender all. We have to say to ourselves, as a society, what we said before the marathon, 'This is as scared as I get – now let's go run'."

MEDALS TABLE
MUNICH 1972 – GAMES OF THE XX OLYMPIAD
SUMMER OLYMPIC GAMES

Nation	Gold	Silver	Bronze	Total
Soviet Union	50	27	22	99
United States	33	31	30	94
East Germany	20	23	23	66
West Germany	13	11	16	40
Japan	13	8	8	29
Australia	8	7	2	17
Poland	7	5	9	21
Hungary	6	13	16	35
Bulgaria	6	10	5	21
Italy	5	3	10	18
Sweden	4	6	6	16
Great Britain	4	5	9	18
Romania	3	6	7	16
Cuba	3	1	4	8
Finland	3	1	4	8
Netherlands	3	1	1	5
France	2	4	7	13
Czechoslovakia	2	4	2	8
Kenya	2	3	4	9
Yugoslavia	2	1	2	5
Norway	2	1	1	4
North Korea	1	1	3	5
New Zealand	1	1	1	3
Uganda	1	1	0	2
Denmark	1	0	0	1
Switzerland	0	3	0	3
Canada	0	2	3	5
Iran	0	2	1	3
Belgium	0	2	0	2
Greece	0	2	0	2
Austria	0	1	2	3
Colombia	0	1	2	3

Nation	Gold	Silver	Bronze	Total
Argentina	0	1	0	1
South Korea	0	1	0	1
Lebanon	0	1	0	1
Mexico	0	1	0	1
Mongolia	0	1	0	1
Pakistan	0	1	0	1
Tunisia	0	1	0	1
Turkey	0	1	0	1
Brazil	0	0	2	2
Ethiopia	0	0	2	2
Ghana	0	0	1	1
India	0	0	1	1
Jamaica	0	0	1	1
Niger	0	0	1	1
Nigeria	0	0	1	1
Spain	0	0	1	1

SPORTS – MUNICH 1972

Events: 195 in 25 sports – Archery | Athletics | Badminton | Basketball | Boxing | Canoeing | Cycling | Diving | Equestrian | Fencing | Football (soccer) | Gymnastics | Handball | Hockey | Judo | Modern pentathlon | Rowing | Sailing | Shooting | Swimming | Volleyball | Water polo | Water skiing | Weightlifting | Wrestling.

CHAPTER 9

1976: Montreal

17 July – 1 August

Games of the XXI Olympiad

Countries participating: 92

Athletes participating:
6,084 (4,824 men, 1,260 women)

Events: 198 in 23 sports

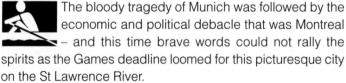 The bloody tragedy of Munich was followed by the economic and political debacle that was Montreal – and this time brave words could not rally the spirits as the Games deadline loomed for this picturesque city on the St Lawrence River.

When, six years earlier, Montreal had first been awarded the 1976 Summer Olympics, Canada's economy was booming. The city immediately embarked on the most ambitious construction programme of breathtaking stadia and other venues.

But by the time the Games arrived, the boom had gone bust in the wake of the 1973 oil crisis. Bad planning, under-budgeting, industrial disputes and a cruelly harsh winter had turned the once-euphoric organisers' dreams into a slow-motion nightmare.

As a defence against any recurrence of the terrorism that had surfaced at Munich, a 16,000-strong security force had been recruited at a cost of at least $100 (Canadian) million. But that was small beer compared with the overall construction bill, which grew from an estimated $310 million to $1.2 billion. Even so, the Olympic Stadium was not completed in time for the start of the Games and the opening ceremony, conducted by Queen Elizabeth, took place in improvised conditions. Cranes still working on the domed roof of the stadium, four miles from downtown Montreal, marred the skyline throughout the events and long after.

As the Games of the XXI Olympiad were launched in the nation's dual languages of English and French, it was ironic that the enthusiastic Games bidders of 1970 had been consigned a crippling debt that its citizens could never repay. Montreal had been awarded the Games because the International Olympic Committee faint-heartedly failed to choose between the principal bidders, who happened to be either side of the Cold War divide: Los Angeles and Moscow. On the second round of voting, the US threw its support behind neighbouring Canada – and landed it with a debt mountain that would scare off other equally deserving but equally penurious bidders for years to come.

As now seemed inevitable, politics afflicted the 1976 Olympics. Thirty countries boycotted Montreal for one reason or another, reducing by about 1,000 the number of competitors compared with Munich. The withdrawals were: Algeria, Cameroon, Central African Republic, Chad, Republic of China, People's Republic of China, Congo, Egypt, Ethiopia, Gabon, Gambia, Ghana, Guyana, Iraq, Kenya, Libya, Madagascar, Malawi, Mali, Morocco, Niger, Nigeria, Sudan, Swaziland, Tanzania, Togo, Tunisia, Uganda, Upper Volta and Zambia. Some announced their decision just 48 hours before the start. Most of the refusals came from African nations, protesting against the inclusion of New Zealand, whose rugby team had recently toured apartheid South Africa.

The Games were also blighted by allegations of drug-taking, few of them ultimately substantiated. Many athletes, especially the East German women swimmers, were accused of using anabolic steroids – on the apparent evidence of their large muscles and deep voices. When Shirley Babashoff of the United States accused her rivals of this malpractice, an East German team official explained: "They came to swim, not to sing." Another interesting aspect of this debate was that Princess Anne, a member of Britain's equestrian team, was the only female competitor not to have to submit to a sex test.

In the midst of all this finger-wagging, name-calling, political posturing, half-built venues and indebted dollars there were heroes and heroines who lifted the spirits.

Alberto Juantorena of Cuba became the first athlete ever to win the

1976: MONTREAL

400 and 800 metres at the same Olympics. The fuzzy-haired giant, nicknamed 'El Caballo' (The Horse) because of his nine-foot stride, set a new world record of 1 minute 43.50 seconds in the 800.

Lasse Viren of Finland duplicated his own feat at the 1972 Munich Olympics by winning the 5,000 and 10,000 metres, the only man in Olympic history to win both events twice. He later competed in the marathon, finishing fifth. Viren, who went on to become a member of the Finnish parliament, was constantly linked with rumours of doping and in between Olympic Games failed to impress. He came fifth in the 10,000 metres in the 1980 Games in Moscow but then dropped out of the marathon after 25 kilometres.

Viktor Saneyev of the Soviet Union won his third consecutive triple-jump gold medal. Klaus Dibiasi of Italy did the same in the platform diving event. The US men's swimming team won all but one gold medal. The East German women's swimming team won all but two gold medals.

Alex Oakley, the Canadian race walker, became the oldest track and field athlete to compete at the Olympic Games. He was aged fifty and taking part in his fifth Olympics.

America's Edwin Moses set a world record in the 400 metre hurdles and Bruce Jenner did the same in the decathlon. Jenner, with his stylishly long hair and boyish good looks, was the golden boy of American track and field in the seventies. He had won twelve out of thirteen decathlons between 1974 and 1976. The Olympics was meant to have seen a close duel between Jenner and the defending champion Mykola Avilov of the Soviet Union but the American was in sparkling form scoring five personal bests on the opening day. He went on to win the gold medal with a world record 8,618 points.

One of the strangest victors was Japanese gymnast Shun Fujimoto, who broke his right leg in the floor exercise but, due to the closeness in the overall standings with the USSR, hid the extent of the injury. In the team championship he completed his event on the rings, performing a perfect triple somersault dismount and maintaining perfect posture. He scored a 9.7 to secure the gold medal for his team.

Another notable Japanese entrant was Taro Aso, a member of the shooting team. Thirty-two years later, he would be elected prime minister of Japan.

The United States entered probably its greatest ever Olympic boxing line-up. Sugar Ray Leonard, Leon Spinks, Michael Spinks, Leo Randolph and Howard Davis Jr won gold medals, and all but Davis went on to become professional world champions. Sugar Ray Leonard, in particular, went on to fame and fortune following his triumph in the light-welterweight class.

Yet the superstar of the entire Games was undoubtedly a fourteen-year-old from Romania, Nadia Comaneci, who dramatically ended the Soviet Union's twenty-year domination of gymnastics.

Comaneci will be forever famous for recording the first perfect '10' on the bars. It was such a shock to the organisers, if not to the ecstatic audience, that the result flashed up on the scoreboard was not a 10 but a 0.1 – because the board had been programmed only up to 9.99. She had not only surpassed her rivals but had beaten Olympic technology. The crowd soon understood the meaning of the score when the memorable announcement was made: "Ladies and gentleman, for the first time in Olympic history, Nadia Comaneci has received the score of a perfect ten."

The tiny 4ft 11in Romanian perhaps lacked the style and charisma that Olga Korbut had shown but the resulting medal tally was unchallengeable. During her magical week in Montreal she earned seven perfect scores: four on the uneven bars and three on the balance beam. She won three gold medals for the all-around competition, uneven bars, and balance beam. She also won a silver medal for the team competition and a bronze medal for the floor exercise.

Nadia Comaneci's performance was the single factor that rescued Montreal from the gloom surrounding the practical and political problems that beset it.

The Games of the XXI Olympiad had begun with memories of a massacre, as the Israeli team entered the opening ceremony with their national flag adorned with a black ribbon. It continued often in embarrassing confusion, summed up when the Olympic flame itself went out. Doused by a rainstorm a few days into the Games, it had to be relit by an official who whipped out his cigarette lighter. Organisers quickly doused it again and relit it using a back-up of the original flame.

The Games ended with the galling image of cranes still hovering over incomplete constructions. Even the Olympic Stadium's much vaunted retractable roof, which had never worked efficiently, finally packed up in 1991, to be replaced with a $25million new one – which itself partly collapsed under the weight of a winter's snow.

The final cost to the Canadian taxpayers was crippling. And what did they have to show for it? Canada finished with five silver and six bronze medals – the first time a host country of the summer Games had failed to win a single gold medal.

MEDALS TABLE
MONTREAL 1976 – GAMES OF THE XXI OLYMPIAD
SUMMER OLYMPIC GAMES

Nation	Gold	Silver	Bronze	Total
Soviet Union	49	41	35	125
East Germany	40	25	25	90
United States	34	35	25	94
West Germany	10	12	17	39
Japan	9	6	10	25
Poland	7	6	13	26
Bulgaria	6	9	7	22
Cuba	6	4	3	13
Romania	4	9	14	27
Hungary	4	5	13	22
Finland	4	2	0	6
Sweden	4	1	0	5
Great Britain	3	5	5	13
Italy	2	7	4	13
France	2	3	4	9
Yugoslavia	2	3	3	8
Czechoslovakia	2	2	4	8
New Zealand	2	1	1	4
South Korea	1	1	4	6
Switzerland	1	1	2	4
Jamaica	1	1	0	2
North Korea	1	1	0	2
Norway	1	1	0	2
Denmark	1	0	2	3
Mexico	1	0	1	2
Trinidad and Tobago	1	0	0	1
Canada	0	5	6	11
Belgium	0	3	3	6
Netherlands	0	2	3	5
Portugal	0	2	0	2
Spain	0	2	0	2
Australia	0	1	4	5
Iran	0	1	1	2

Nation	Gold	Silver	Bronze	Total
Mongolia	0	1	0	1
Venezuela	0	1	0	1
Brazil	0	0	2	2
Austria	0	0	1	1
Bermuda	0	0	1	1
Pakistan	0	0	1	1
Puerto Rico	0	0	1	1
Thailand	0	0	1	1

SPORTS – MONTREAL 1976

Events: 198 in 23 sports – Archery | Athletics | Basketball | Boxing | Canoeing | Cycling | Diving | Equestrian | Fencing | Football | Gymnastics | Handball | Hockey | Judo | Modern pentathlon | Rowing | Sailing | Shooting | Swimming | Volleyball | Water polo | Weightlifting | Wrestling.

CHAPTER 10

1980: Moscow

19 July – 3 August

Games of the XXII Olympiad

Countries participating: 80

Athletes participating:
5,179 athletes (4,064 men, 1,115 women)

Events: 203 in 23 sports

 The idealistic argument that politics should under no circumstances be allowed to interfere with the Olympic Games took its severest battering in 1980. The Cold War saw to that. Coming after the terrorist atrocity in Munich and the financial disaster of Montreal, the political turmoil surrounding Moscow appeared to many observers to be the final nail in the coffin of the Olympic Games.

The catalyst was the Soviet Union's invasion of Afghanistan at Christmas 1979. Many Western nations instantly tried to organise boycotts of the Moscow Games in protest. As the opening ceremony loomed, the growing list of absentees seemed endless. But it was the non-appearances of the USA that made the most significant difference to the validity of the Games of the XXII Olympiad.

Juan Antonio Samaranch had only just taken up his post as IOC president, an organisation in financial crisis in the 1970s, and with Los Angeles set to host the 1984 Games, more boycotting from the Soviet bloc was inevitable. Could the Olympics survive?

A GUIDE TO THE OLYMPIC GAMES AND LONDON 2012

In the end only 80 nations turned up in Moscow, a reduction of 42 on the highest previous attendance, 121 at Munich in 1972. The absentees included Canada, Kenya, West Germany, Japan, Turkey and Israel. The US boycott was personally directed by President Jimmy Carter. Ironically, Afghanistan did send a team – and the American ban did not extend to a trade boycott with the USSR. This encouraged many sportsmen in their belief that an Olympic embargo was an easier option for governments than a trade embargo and that their aspirations were being sacrificed in a pointless gesture.

Britain's Prime Minister Margaret Thatcher supported the USA and pressed athletes to stay at home. She sent a series of letters to the British Olympic Association warning it would be "against British interests and wrong" for them to compete. In one, she urged: "The Games will serve the propaganda needs of the Soviet Government. There is no effective palliative, such as cutting out the ceremonies. I remain firmly convinced that it is neither in our national interest nor in the wider Western interest for Britain to take part in the Games in Moscow. As a sporting event, the Games cannot now satisfy the aspirations of our sportsmen and women. British attendance in Moscow can only serve to frustrate the interests of Britain."

The British Government targeted athletes who worked in the civil service, refusing them permission to attend but they could not stop any other athletes competing if they so wished. Disclosures released under the Official Secrets Act three decades later showed that Britain's golden hope, Sebastian Coe, had led a defiant campaign of refusal to toe the government line. His decision to compete in Moscow has since been recognised as a defining moment within the Olympic movement.

Many nations, including Britain, decided to stage their own protests, such as marching under the Olympic flag or replacing their own national anthems at medal ceremonies with the Olympic hymn. Despite the boycott the standard in all events was extremely high. Officially opened by Leonid Brezhnev, the organisation of the Games could barely be faulted, apart from the heavy-handed security arrangements.

The most anticipated contests were the 800 metres and 1500 metres. These were events in which one of the most hyped clashes in Olympic history took place in the magnificent 100,000-capacity Lenin Stadium: the duel between Sebastian Coe and Steve Ovett. The British middle-distance heroes had been individually trading world records on the European circuit without either of them testing themselves against the other.

1980: MOSCOW

Coe was the world record holder over 800 metres but Ovett led the field, with Coe trailing at the back and leaving it too late to make up for lost time. Ovett triumphed in 1 minute 45.40 seconds, with his countryman coming second. Coe described it as "the worst tactical race of my life".

Six days later the tables were turned – when again the 'wrong' man won his opponent's speciality. This time Ovett was the favourite as they met in the final of the 1,500 metres. Running the perfect race this time, Coe sped around the last bend leaving Ovett in third place behind East Germany's Jurgen Straub. Coe had covered the last 400 metres in 52.2 seconds and the last 100 metres in 12.1 seconds, the fastest-ever finish at this distance. For disappointed Ovett it was his first defeat in forty-five races over either 1,500 metres or a mile.

The 100 metres was the narrowest of wins for Allan Wells, who became the first Briton to win the event in fifty-six years. He beat Silvio Leonard of Cuba in the final stride, although both were given the same time. To complete an exceptional Games achievement for Britain, Daley Thompson won the decathlon.

Ethiopia's Miruts Yifter earned the affectionate nickname 'Yifter the Shifter' after his golden double at the Moscow Olympics. He won the 5,000 metres and 10,000 metres, both with blistering sprint finishes over the final 300 metres. It was a remarkable repeat of Lasse Viren's 5,000 and 10,000 metres double in Munich.

Meanwhile, East Germany's Waldemar Cierpinski became only the second man to have won two Olympic marathon titles (Abebe Bikila in 1960 and 1964, Cierpinski in 1976 and 1980). In Moscow, Cierpinski finished in 2 hours 11 minutes 3 seconds. He might have aspired to a record third win in Los Angeles four years later but that was to be made impossible by the Eastern Bloc's predictable tit-for-tat boycott.

Less popular visitors from East Germany were the nation's female swimmers, despite winning twenty-six of the possible thirty-five medals – the reason being their suspiciously gruff voices and masculine appearance. Many years later it was confirmed they had all been on drugs supplied by their communist state trainers.

Another communist victory was deservedly secured by the giant Cuban boxer Teofilo Stevenson, who once again took the Olympic heavyweight gold medal – becoming the first man to win the same event in three Games, betwixt 1972 and 1980.

After two Olympics in which tiny girl gymnasts had produced the most spellbinding performances, Moscow's star of the gymnastics hall was not a woman but a man. Russia's Aleksandr Dityatin won a record eight medals and his maximum 10 in the horse vault was the first ever awarded to a male gymnast.

Four years earlier the star on the bars had been 14-year-old Romanian Nadia Comaneci. In Moscow she took two gold medals before deciding to quit athletics at the age of nineteen. Shortly afterwards she was forced to deny that she had had an affair with Nicu Ceausescu, son of the tyrannical Romanian dictator. In 1989 after several attempts to emigrate to the West, she walked six hours in darkness to cross the Hungarian border, from where she escaped to the USA.

And that is pretty much how many of the visiting media corps felt after covering the Moscow Olympic Games. Having tussled with officialdom, suffered an unpredictable communications service and having been harassed by strong-arm security while trying to cover the various human rights protests that were taking place in Moscow, liberty beckoned four years down the line … when the Games would move to the 'Land of the Free'.

MEDALS TABLE
MOSCOW 1980 – GAMES OF THE XXII OLYMPIAD
SUMMER OLYMPIC GAMES

Nation	Gold	Silver	Bronze	Total
Soviet Union	80	69	46	195
East Germany	47	37	42	126
Bulgaria	8	16	17	41
Cuba	8	7	5	20
Italy	8	3	4	15
Hungary	7	10	15	32
Romania	6	6	13	25
France	6	5	3	14
Great Britain	5	7	9	21
Poland	3	14	15	32
Sweden	3	3	6	12
Finland	3	1	4	8
Czechoslovakia	2	3	9	14
Yugoslavia	2	3	4	9
Australia	2	2	5	9
Denmark	2	1	2	5
Brazil	2	0	2	4
Ethiopia	2	0	2	4
Switzerland	2	0	0	2
Spain	1	3	2	6
Austria	1	2	1	4
Greece	1	0	2	3
Belgium	1	0	0	1
India	1	0	0	1
Zimbabwe	1	0	0	1
North Korea	0	3	2	5
Mongolia	0	2	2	4
Tanzania	0	2	0	2
Mexico	0	1	3	4
Netherlands	0	1	2	3
Ireland	0	1	1	2
Uganda	0	1	0	1
Venezuela	0	1	0	1

Nation	Gold	Silver	Bronze	Total
Jamaica	0	0	3	3
Guyana	0	0	1	1
Lebanon	0	0	1	1

SPORTS – MOSCOW 1980

Events: 203 in 23 sports – Archery | Athletics | Basketball | Boxing | Canoeing | Cycling | Diving | Equestrian | Fencing | Football | Gymnastics | Handball | Hockey | Judo | Modern pentathlon | Rowing | Sailing | Shooting | Swimming | Volleyball | Water polo | Weightlifting | Wrestling.

CHAPTER **11**

1984: Los Angeles

28 July – 12 August

Games of the XXIII Olympiad

Countries participating: 140

Athletes participating:
6,829 (5,263 men; 1,566 women)

Events: 221 in 26 sports

The Americans achieved in 1984 what no other host nation had managed in the recent history of the Games... they turned a profit. Learning the lessons of financially-strapped Montreal, when the Olympics returned to the North American continent it was with the backing of corporate sponsors. Forty-three companies were licensed to sell official Olympic products. So, although the Games were as lavishly staged as befitted their Californian setting, it managed to notch up a $225 million profit – the first time the figures had climbed out of the red since 1932. And those Games, of course, had also been set in Los Angeles.

It is not overstating the case that LA '84, officially opened on 28 July by President Ronald Reagan, may truly be judged as the salvation of the Olympic Games. And yet it could have been yet another nail-biting disappointment due to last-minute 'refuseniks'. To no-one's surprise the Soviet Union retaliated for the American-led 1980 boycott of Moscow by staying away – and keeping most of its Eastern Bloc satellites away, too. The tit-for-tat decision was announced on the very day that the Olympic flame arrived on American soil, with the USSR claiming that their athletes were being withdrawn because the US could not guarantee their safety. Only Romania among the Eastern Bloc countries failed to toe the communist line and sent a delegation.

Yet another disaster was forecast but a mixture of free-world fighting spirit, unbounded patriotism and a string of memorable athletic performances turned the Los Angeles Olympics into what many deemed to be the most successful in the history of the Games.

There was a fourth magic ingredient that helped convince the world that the Games was worth saving: capitalist cash. Television rights to the events brought in $287 million as the spectacle was beamed to an estimated 2,500 million people around the world, one of the largest TV audiences in history.

What they saw on their box-like television sets was a stunning spectacle from the very start, centred on the 92,000-seat Memorial Coliseum, which had been the site of the 1932 Games but had been fully refurbished.

What had also changed in the intervening half-century was the scale. When it had last staged the Olympic Games, Los Angeles had attracted 1,332 athletes (1,206 men and 126 women) from thirty-seven nations contesting 116 events in fourteen just sports. On 28 July 1984, no fewer than 6,797 athletes (5,230 men and 1,567 women) from 140 nations were about to take part in 221 events in twenty-six sports.

When the Olympic torch entered the stadium, it was in the hand of Gina Hemphill, great granddaughter of the great Jesse Owens. She handed over the torch to Rafer Johnson, the 1960 Olympic decathlon champion, who lit the flame on top of the stadium peristyle by means of a ninety-six-step hydraulic stairway. The opening ceremony that followed was a three-hour Hollywood-style extravaganza that set the tone for the rest of the Games.

The Games also produced some of the greatest athletic prowess in history – and here the name Jesse Owens came up again. For his feat in Munich forty-eight years earlier was now matched in Los Angeles by the quadruple gold medal performance of one of the greatest athletes in history, Carl Lewis. The tall, long-legged Lewis won golds in the 100 metres, 200 metres, the long jump and the 4 x 100 metres relay.

1984: LOS ANGELES

Despite these triumphs Lewis was not the most popular contestant among press, officials and sometimes spectators. Judged a flamboyant show-off he petulantly complained at the treatment of athletes, turned up late for press conferences and, in the long jump, was booed for passing on his final four jumps to conserve his energy – thereby failing to challenge Bob Beamon's then world record of 8.9 metres.

The greatest controversy of the Games, however, was over the result of the women's 3,000 metres in which American favourite Mary Decker tangled with barefoot Zola Budd, an eighteen-year-old South African running under British colours.

Budd had already suffered criticism after her application for British citizenship had been fast-tracked in time for her to compete at the Games. As a South African she would have been ineligible, and the decision to enter her in a British 'vest of convenience' had infuriated anti-apartheid campaigners.

Now, running barefoot in the women's 3,000 metres final, the teenager horrified the crowd by appearing to trip twenty-six-year-old Decker, putting the popular American out of the race. The incident occurred shortly after the half-way mark when, with Budd slightly in front, she and Decker bumped into each other twice, causing the diminutive South African to stumble and trip her rival.

Decker pitched forward and crashed to the ground, clutching her right thigh. She was carried from the track in tears as Budd raced on. The hostile American crowd began booing, which so unnerved Budd that she could finish only seventh, and Maricica Puica of Romania took the gold. After initially disqualifying Budd for obstruction, she was reinstated just one hour later after officials had viewed footage of the race.

A more popular British performance on the track was by one of the nation's top Moscow champions, Seb Coe. But a hoped-for repeat of his sporting clash with countryman Steve Ovett never materialised. With a gold medal apiece from 1980, each having won in the other's favourite event, Los Angeles effectively signalled the end of their rivalry.

Coe missed out on the 800 metre gold medal and had to settle for a bronze, beaten by Brazil's Joaquim Cruz and new British rival Steve Cram. Ovett finished last after struggling with a virus and the notorious Los Angeles pollution. He collapsed after the race and spent two days in hospital.

Ovett returned for the 1,500 metres but was forced to pull out on the final lap when lying in fourth place. That allowed Coe to become the only man to win a second successive 1,500 metre final, outpacing Cram in an Olympic record 3 minutes 32.53 seconds. This was an even more remarkable victory because Coe had spent the past year recovering from a blood disorder.

The other repeat British hero of Moscow and Los Angeles was Daley Thompson, who retained his title in the decathlon. The thick-set, 195-pound six-footer was competing against Jurgen Hingsen, who had taken over from him as the world record holder. Thompson not only beat the West German but equalled Hingsen's world record. It was a hugely popular victory by a man who – with four world records, two Olympic gold medals, three Commonwealth titles, and wins in the World Championships and the European Championships – has often been described as 'the world's greatest decathlete'.

However, most medals by far went to the host country. Helped by the Eastern Bloc boycott, the US won eighty-three golds. Next came Romania, with twenty.

One of the biggest thrills for the home fans, accustomed to seeing the gymnastic crown going to East Europeans like Olga Korbut and Nadia Comaneci, was the sight of an American girl stealing the show. She was Mary Lou Retton who became the first US woman to win the all-round gymnastics gold. The effervescent sixteen-year-old performed stunning flips and a perfect 10 vault, displayed not once but twice with equal precision, becoming the first American woman to earn a gold medal in gymnastics.

Equally amazing was Joan Benoit's victory in the inaugural women's marathon. Two weeks before the compulsory trial race she needed arthroscopic surgery on her right knee. She recovered sufficiently to win the trial in just over two-and-a-half hours. In the marathon itself Bemoit took a commanding lead after only three miles and stayed way ahead of the rest of the field, including world champion Grete Waitz, finishing in 2 hours 24 minutes 52 seconds.

The People's Republic of China participated in the Summer Games for the first time since 1952. Li Ning won six medals in gymnastics: three gold, two silver and a bronze.

One less than savoury record was broken at Los Angeles. A shamed twelve competitors were disqualified after testing positive for performance-enhancing drugs, including Finland's 10,000 metres silver medallist Martti Vainio. Several other positive tests were unpublicised.

1984: LOS ANGELES

By the time the Californian spectacular ended on 12 August, total attendances had topped a remarkable 5.7 million, the largest crowd being for the football final at the Pasadena Rose Bowl where 101,799 spectators watched France beat Brazil.

One enduring theme of the XXIII Olympics was the work of John Williams – not an athlete but a composer. He won a Grammy award for his music, which has since become a signature of the Games: 'Olympic Fanfare and Theme'.

MEDALS TABLE
LOS ANGELES 1984 – GAMES OF THE XXIII OLYMPIAD
SUMMER OLYMPIC GAMES

Nation	Gold	Silver	Bronze	Total
United States	83	61	30	174
Romania	20	16	17	53
West Germany	17	19	23	59
China	15	8	9	32
Italy	14	6	12	32
Canada	10	18	16	44
Japan	10	8	14	32
New Zealand	8	1	2	11
Yugoslavia	7	4	7	18
South Korea	6	6	7	19
Great Britain	5	11	21	37
France	5	7	16	28
Netherlands	5	2	6	13
Australia	4	8	12	24
Finland	4	2	6	12
Sweden	2	11	6	19
Mexico	2	3	1	6
Morocco	2	0	0	2
Brazil	1	5	2	8
Spain	1	2	2	5
Belgium	1	1	2	4
Austria	1	1	1	3
Kenya	1	0	2	3
Portugal	1	0	2	3
Pakistan	1	0	0	1
Switzerland	0	4	4	8
Denmark	0	3	3	6
Jamaica	0	1	2	3
Norway	0	1	2	3
Greece	0	1	1	2
Nigeria	0	1	1	2
Puerto Rico	0	1	1	2
Colombia	0	1	0	1

1984: LOS ANGELES

Nation	Gold	Silver	Bronze	Total
Côte d'Ivoire	0	1	0	1
Egypt	0	1	0	1
Ireland	0	1	0	1
Peru	0	1	0	1
Syria	0	1	0	1
Thailand	0	1	0	1
Turkey	0	0	3	3
Venezuela	0	0	3	3
Algeria	0	0	2	2
Cameroon	0	0	1	1
Chinese Taipei	0	0	1	1
Dominican Republic	0	0	1	1
Iceland	0	0	1	1
Zambia	0	0	1	1

SPORTS – LOS ANGELES 1984

Events: 221 in 26 sports - Archery | Athletics | Baseball | Basketball | Boxing | Canoeing | Cycling | Diving | Equestrian | Fencing | Football | Gymnastics | Handball | Hockey | Judo | Modern pentathlon | Rowing | Sailing | Shooting | Swimming | Synchronized swimming | Tennis | Volleyball | Water polo | Weightlifting | Wrestling.

CHAPTER **12**

1988: Seoul

17 September – 2 October

Games of the XXIV Olympiad

Countries participating: 159

Athletes participating:
8,391 (6,197 men, 2,194 women)

Events: 237 in 28 sports

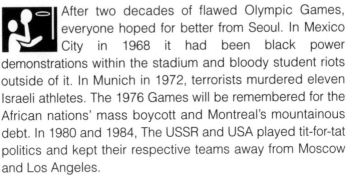

After two decades of flawed Olympic Games, everyone hoped for better from Seoul. In Mexico City in 1968 it had been black power demonstrations within the stadium and bloody student riots outside of it. In Munich in 1972, terrorists murdered eleven Israeli athletes. The 1976 Games will be remembered for the African nations' mass boycott and Montreal's mountainous debt. In 1980 and 1984, The USSR and USA played tit-for-tat politics and kept their respective teams away from Moscow and Los Angeles.

So what could go wrong in Seoul, South Korea, in 1988? Quite a lot, it seemed. With South and North Korea technically at war and the demilitarised zone separating the two just thirty-five miles away, the South's capital seemed tragically well placed for another superpower confrontation.

North Korea's first salvo was to demand that it co-host the entire Games. Pressure mounted when the North was accused by the South of being behind two fatal bombings. The International Olympic Committee tried unsuccessfully to negotiate a settlement before letting it be known that they would cancel rather than switch the Summer Olympics if political problems made it impossible to hold them in South Korea. "It is Seoul or no 1988 Olympics," said IOC president Juan Antonio Samaranch. "Either we go to Seoul or there will be no Games."

North Korea's brinksmanship ultimately failed as East-West relations began to thaw and the threat of large-scale boycotts along the pattern of Moscow and Los Angeles melted away. In the end all but four nations – North Korea, Cuba, Ethiopia and Nicaragua – failed to send teams to Seoul, compared with the 159 nations that chose to enter. Thus the USSR and USA were able to compete against one another for the first time in twelve years.

If the politics that had dogged the Olympics for decades now seemed to be at an end, another shameful cloud was set to blight the XXIV Olympiad – the Games that will forever be remembered for drug scandals. The Games were also marred by cheating, bad manners and temper tantrums but it was the scourge of drugs for which Seoul will, sadly, be remembered.

Bulgarian weightlifters Mitko Grablev and Angel Guenchev had their gold medals removed for using banned substances and several other minor athletes were disqualified by the IOC, including a Hungarian silver-medal weightlifter and a British bronze-medal judoist.

But the biggest drugs bust of all shamed a man who had briefly been the greatest hero of the Games: Ben Johnson. The twenty-six-year-old Canadian sprinter had dramatically won the 100 metres beating his archrival, Carl Lewis of the US, in world-record time of 9.79 seconds. Graciously handing the gold medal to his mother Gloria, he won the hearts of the crowd by saying: "I won the gold for her." Three days later he had to ask her for it back.

A 2am knock on his bedroom door brought the Canadian's glorious career to an ignominious end. Johnson's coach woke him to tell him he was to be stripped of his record because he had tested positive for the anabolic steroid stanozolol. As Johnson flew home in disgrace the entire sixty-four-strong Canadian track and field team volunteered themselves for mass testing, though Olympic officials refused the offer.

Even when feats of amazing athleticism were performed the suspicion that drugs might be behind the victories soured proceedings. A case in point was the amazing successes of glamorous Florence Griffith Joyner, who rewrote the record books with a series of unexpected performances.

1988: SEOUL

Flo Jo, as she became known, won the 100 metres in 10.54 seconds and set two world records at 200 metres in 21.34 seconds. She won a further gold in the 4 x 200 metres relay, adding a silver in the 4 x 400 metres relay, in which she ran a 48.07 seconds leg. She also ran the fastest ever Olympic time over 100 metres, although this was judged to have been wind assisted.

The problem was that the super-sprinter had not previously shown such superlative prowess. Joyner was wife of the 1984 Olympic triple-jump winner Al Joyner and the sister-in-law of the 1984 and 1988 heptathlon champion Jackie Joyner Kersee. But her sporting pedigree did not explain the flamboyant twenty-seven-year-old's sudden leap in performance to become top athlete of the Games, and accusations consequently flew that she was using anabolic steroids and human growth hormone. She denied the allegations – right up to her sudden death from a heart attack at the early age of thirty-eight.

Another American became the instant centre of attention at the Games for entirely different reasons. Regarded as one of the greatest divers of all time, Greg Louganis had been just sixteen when he qualified for the 1976 Games in Montreal, where he finished sixth in the springboard event and won a silver medal in the platform. The US boycott kept him away from Moscow but in Los Angeles he won both springboard and platform golds.

Now, in Seoul, he repeated that double win but only after an alarming incident in the springboard qualifier when he misjudged a reverse two-and-a-half somersault in the pike position and cracked his head on the board. A doctor swiftly stitched up the wound but Louganis, who had been diagnosed as HIV positive six months before, and was misguidedly fearful that blood spilled in the pool could infect other competitors.

Among other American notables, Carl Lewis retained his gold medals for the long jump and 100 metres, both of which he had won four years earlier in Los Angeles (along with the 200 metres and 4 x 100 metres relay).

But it was the Iron Curtain countries that made perhaps the greatest impression at Seoul. They came storming back to the Games after their Los Angeles boycott and knocked the US into third slot in the honours with ninety-four medals, thirty-six of them golds. That compared with East Germany's 102 medals (thirty-seven of them golds) and the Soviet Union's top tally of 132 medals (fifty-five gold).

In swimming events, Americans put up a creditable performance, with Matt Biondi winning five golds, a silver and a bronze and team-mate Janet Evans taking three golds. But it was an East German, Kristin Otto, who dominated this field, coming first in every event she entered, thereby attaining six gold medals, the most ever won by a female in Olympic history.

Like her countryfolk, Otto had missed the Los Angeles Games and this, compounded by the fact that the Eastern Bloc was still a closed community, made her victories even more unheralded. The tall, sturdy twenty-two-year-old took three 100 metres titles in butterfly, backstroke and freestyle, adding golds in 50 metres freestyle and 4 x 100 metres freestyle and medley relays. Her achievement put her tantalisingly close to Mark Spitz's 1972 record. But her reputation was somewhat tarnished by later revelations that she, like other East German swimmers, had (possibly unknowingly) been fed banned substances, including testosterone, throughout her youthful career.

Of course there were highlights of the Seoul Olympics that remained untarnished. The addition of tennis as a medal-winning sport (as opposed to a demonstration sport) brought to the Games a level of professionalism as well as nail-biting suspense. Czechoslovakia's Miloslav Mecir won the men's singles but West German woman champion Steffi Graf of West Germany was the sport's first Olympic superstar.

Graf, who incidentally had been an outstanding 800 metres runner as a girl, was destined to be the world's female number one on the court for almost the whole of the next decade. But it was the year 1998 that established her as a tennis phenomenon when she became only the fifth player in history, of either sex, to win the Grand Slam, taking Wimbledon and the Australian, French and US Opens in the same year. Her performance at Seoul topped even that when she became the first and only tennis player to achieve what was termed the 'Golden Slam' by adding a gold medal to her four singles victories within the same calendar year.

The fact that Graf and her fellow players were there at all was doubly significant. Tennis had not featured at the Olympics since 1924 when it was eliminated because of the amateur rule that had confused officials and hampered athletes since the inception of the modern Games. When the rule was finally overturned in 1986 it fell to individual sports bodies to determine whether or not professionals should be allowed to compete. This derestriction allowed tennis to return to the Olympic Games.

1988: SEOUL

For that reason alone Seoul was a ground-breaking Olympics. It was also significant for South Korea's ambitious and successful construction of an entire new Olympia, a blueprint that cities around the world have since followed. And it was in this purpose-built Olympia that politics seemed at last to have been put aside and, despite the blemish of drugs, the Olympic Games advanced to a new level of national sporting pride and professionalism.

MEDALS TABLE
SEOUL 1988 – GAMES OF THE XXIV OLYMPIAD
SUMMER OLYMPIC GAMES

Nation	Gold	Silver	Bronze	Total
Soviet Union	55	31	46	132
East Germany	37	35	30	102
United States	36	31	27	94
South Korea	12	10	11	33
West Germany	11	14	15	40
Hungary	11	6	6	23
Bulgaria	10	12	13	35
Romania	7	11	6	24
France	6	4	6	16
Italy	6	4	4	14
China	5	11	12	28
Great Britain	5	10	9	24
Kenya	5	2	2	9
Japan	4	3	7	14
Australia	3	6	5	14
Yugoslavia	3	4	5	12
Czechoslovakia	3	3	2	8
New Zealand	3	2	8	13
Canada	3	2	5	10
Poland	2	5	9	16
Norway	2	3	0	5
Netherlands	2	2	5	9
Denmark	2	1	1	4
Brazil	1	2	3	6
Finland	1	1	2	4
Spain	1	1	2	4
Turkey	1	1	0	2
Morocco	1	0	2	3
Austria	1	0	0	1
Portugal	1	0	0	1
Suriname	1	0	0	1
Sweden	0	4	7	11
Switzerland	0	2	2	4

1988: SEOUL

Nation	Gold	Silver	Bronze	Total
Jamaica	0	2	0	2
Argentina	0	1	1	2
Chile	0	1	0	1
Costa Rica	0	1	0	1
Indonesia	0	1	0	1
Iran	0	1	0	1
Netherlands Antilles	0	1	0	1
Peru	0	1	0	1
Senegal	0	1	0	1
Virgin Islands	0	1	0	1
Belgium	0	0	2	2
Mexico	0	0	2	2
Colombia	0	0	1	1
Djibouti	0	0	1	1
Greece	0	0	1	1
Mongolia	0	0	1	1
Pakistan	0	0	1	1
Philippines	0	0	1	1
Thailand	0	0	1	1

SPORTS – SEOUL 1988

Events: 237 in 28 sports – Archery | Athletics | Baseball | Basketball | Boxing | Canoeing | Cycling | Diving | Equestrian | Fencing | Football | Gymnastics | Handball | Hockey | Judo | Modern pentathlon | Rowing | Sailing | Shooting | Swimming | Synchronized swimming | Table tennis | Tennis | Volleyball | Water polo | Weightlifting | Wrestling | Taekwondo.

CHAPTER 13

1992: Barcelona

25 July – 9 August

Games of the XXV Olympiad

Countries participating: 169

Athletes participating:
9,356 (6,652 men, 2,704 women)

Events: 257 in 30 sports

 Unity was the enduringly memorable theme of the Barcelona Olympics, summed up by one unplanned but amazingly symbolic event. South Africa had been allowed to compete in these Games after a thirty-two-year suspension over its apartheid policy. In the 10,000 metres, white South African Elana Meyer and black Ethiopian Derartu Tulu ran a fantastically close race. Tulu, a former shepherdess, ultimately finished ahead. The pair then ran a most moving victory lap hand in hand.

There were many other demonstrations of unity throughout these Games of the XXV Olympiad...

Closest to home was the effect the Games had on the historic enmity between Catalonia, of which Barcelona is capital, and the rest of Spain under the national government in Madrid. In bringing the Games to his Catalan homeland, IOC president Juan Antonio Samaranch eased an often virulent and sometimes violent rivalry that had existed since the Spanish Civil War of the 1930s. The subjugated Catalans had continued to defend their independence of language and spirit but the arrival of the XXV Olympics served to unify them with the rest of their countrymen.

On the wider world stage the Games, the first in three decades without a boycott, saw athletes from most of the new countries of the former Soviet Union compete as the 'Unified Team', although the Baltic nations of Estonia, Latvia and Lithuania opted to send their own contingents. Likewise, the break-up of communist Yugoslavia led to the debuts of Croatia, Slovenia and Herzegovina. With the Berlin Wall demolished in 1990, Barcelona also saw the re-emergence of Germany as a genuinely one-nation team.

There was significance in Israel's successes in Barcelona. Yael Arad became the first Israeli to win an Olympic medal, earning a silver in women's half-middleweight judo. The following day Oren Smadja became Israel's first male medalist, winning a bronze in the same sport. This was noteworthy because their performances coincided with the twentieth anniversary of the Munich massacre and the 500th anniversary of the so-called Alhambra Decree, whereby the Jews were expelled from Catholic Spain in 1492.

Women's judo had been newly introduced to the Olympic programme as had badminton, while slalom canoeing returned after a twenty-year absence. But the exciting breakthrough was that baseball, a demonstration sport in earlier Games, was also added to the Olympic roster. The amateur rule that had been overturned for the 1988 Olympics, allowed the United States to send its 'Dream Team' made up of some of the most famous professional competitors, including the multi-million-dollar celebrities of the NBA. The result was that stars like Michael Jordan, Magic Johnson and Larry Bird vanquished the opposition and won the gold medal by an average of forty points a game.

Professionalism and investment were in evidence at every stage of the Barcelona Games. The Spanish poured money into the preparations for the Olympics, both in infrastructure and training. The cost, reckoned to top £5 billion, went mainly on the many new and refurbished stadia. But money was also lavishly spent on the athletes themselves. Government agencies and leading corporate sponsors devoted funds approaching £200 million to training programmes. Added to that were trust funds set up in advance for each gold medal winner.

Coaches were hired from around the world – from the former Soviet Union for archery and cycling, from Cuba for boxing and volleyball, from Bulgaria for weightlifting, Hungary in fencing, Croatia for water polo and

1992: BARCELONA

from Britain for the equestrian events. More than £500,000 was put aside to train a horse named 'Fino Barcelona '92'in the equestrian events. Embarrassingly, it finished nineteenth.

More fleet of hoof were the Spanish athletes whose high-priced training earned dividends, with thirteen gold medals in Barcelona. Until 1992, Spain had won only four golds in the history of the Summer Olympics. The victory of Fermin Cacho Ruiz in the 1,500 metres was among the more spectacular. Not considered a serious contender, he positioned himself cleverly for a leap forward in the final lap, sprinting past the leaders in the stretch to steal the gold in 3 minutes 40.12 seconds.

The medals were well spread across the international spectrum – although gymnast Vitaly Sherbo of Belarus notched up six of the gold variety, including four on a single day. Sherbo, representing the Unified Team, won five of the six golds in individual events, tying with the record for individual gold medals at a single Olympics set by American speed skater Eric Heiden at the 1980 Winter Games in Lake Placid, New York. It would not be until the 2008 Summer Games in Beijing that US swimmer Michael Phelps equalled this record. Sherbo competed at Barcelona wearing the hammer-and-sickle symbol of the Soviet Union. It wasn't a political statement, he explained, but a sign of his gratitude to the state system that moulded him as a champion.

Another breakthrough in the tally of individual golds came in the diminutive form of Krisztina Egerszegi, known as the 'Hungarian Mouse'. Four years earlier in Seoul, when aged just fourteen years and forty days, she had become the youngest swimmer to win an Olympic gold. Now, in Barcelona, she retained her 200 metres backstroke title with the second fastest time in history and an Olympic record. To that feat she added the 100 metres backstroke and the 400 metres medley titles. And all these were just preliminary events to the astonishing success she was to have four years later in Atlanta.

America's graceful multiple champion Carl Lewis was another highly anticipated victor. Back in 1984 he had wowed his Los Angeles audience with four golds in the 100 and 200 metres, the long jump and the 4 x 100 metres relay – thus emulating his hero, the great Jesse Owens. Four years later in Seoul he had retained his 100 metres and long jump titles. Now, in Barcelona he won his third consecutive long jump gold medal and anchored the US 400 metres relay to a world record.

Other Americans who shone included Evelyn Ashford, who won her fourth Olympic gold medal in the 4 x 100 metres relay – one of only four female athletes to have achieved this. Gail Devers, who almost lost her feet to a blood disorder, won the women's 100 metres in one of the closest races in history, with five runners finishing within 0.06 seconds of each other. Jackie Joyner-Kersee repeated her 1988 victory in the heptathlon, helping the gracefully powerful athlete to her career tally of six Olympic medals, including her two heptathlon golds and a1988 long jump gold, plus four world titles.

British runner Derek Redmond memorably won a standing ovation from the crowd – without even being in sight of a medal. Redmond, whose career had been blighted by a series of injuries, tore a hamstring during a 400 metres semi-final heat. As he struggled to finish, fighting back the pain, his father entered the track without credentials and, with the crowd in uproarious support, helped him complete the race. The familial fortitude became the subject of an IOC video celebrating the Olympic spirit and was used in advertisements by Visa and Nike.

Another 'golden oldie' at the Games was Britain's Linford Christie, who decided on one last bid for Olympic glory at the age of thirty-two and became the oldest man in history to win the 100 metres title. Never accused of a lack of confidence, Christie explained: "I'm the best. I am a remarkable athlete." That boast was only proven after a shaky start for the Jamaican-born Briton. Ignoring his training schedule, Christie failed to make Britain's team for the 1984 Los Angeles Olympics, even in the sprint relay. But the shock of rejection spurred him to dedicated efforts over the next decade, earning him a record twenty-three major championship medals, of which ten were gold.

In Seoul in 1988 his Olympics dream drew closer when he was promoted to the silver medal behind Carl Lewis after the shamed Ben Johnson lost a drugs test and his title. The elusive global gold seemed beyond Christie and he threatened more than once to quit. But deciding to take one last bid at Olympic glory, he at last won the genuine accolades 'Britain's greatest ever sprinter' and 'the world's fastest man' when he blazed down the Barcelona track to win the 100 metres title.

By the time the Games of the XXV Olympiad drew to a close, to the sound of 'Amigos Para Siempre' (Friends For Life) sung by Sarah Brightman and José Carreras, the billions invested in Barcelona had repaid dividends not only in spectacle, athleticism and honours but in the infrastructure, life-quality and reputation of a historic city. The Barcelona Games left not only a more united nation but a less fragmented world.

MEDALS TABLE
BARCELONA 1992 – GAMES OF THE XXV OLYMPIAD
SUMMER OLYMPIC GAMES

Nation	Gold	Silver	Bronze	Total
Unified Team	45	38	29	112
United States	37	34	37	108
Germany	33	21	28	82
China	16	22	16	54
Cuba	14	6	11	31
Spain	13	7	2	22
South Korea	12	5	12	29
Hungary	11	12	7	30
France	8	5	16	29
Australia	7	9	11	27
Canada	7	4	7	18
Italy	6	5	8	19
Great Britain	5	3	12	20
Romania	4	6	8	18
Czechoslovakia	4	2	1	7
North Korea	4	0	5	9
Japan	3	8	11	22
Bulgaria	3	7	6	16
Poland	3	6	10	19
Netherlands	2	6	7	15
Kenya	2	4	2	8
Norway	2	4	1	7
Turkey	2	2	2	6
Indonesia	2	2	1	5
Brazil	2	1	0	3
Greece	2	0	0	2
Sweden	1	7	4	12
New Zealand	1	4	5	10
Finland	1	2	2	5
Denmark	1	1	4	6
Morocco	1	1	1	3
Ireland	1	1	0	2
Ethiopia	1	0	2	3
Algeria	1	0	1	2

Nation	Gold	Silver	Bronze	Total
Estonia	1	0	1	2
Lithuania	1	0	1	2
Switzerland	1	0	0	1
Jamaica	0	3	1	4
Nigeria	0	3	1	4
Latvia	0	2	1	3
Austria	0	2	0	2
Namibia	0	2	0	2
South Africa	0	2	0	2
Belgium	0	1	2	3
Croatia	0	1	2	3
Independent Olympic Participants	0	1	2	3
Iran	0	1	2	3
Israel	0	1	1	2
Chinese Taipei	0	1	0	1
Mexico	0	1	0	1
Peru	0	1	0	1
Mongolia	0	0	2	2
Slovenia	0	0	2	2
Argentina	0	0	1	1
Bahamas	0	0	1	1
Colombia	0	0	1	1
Ghana	0	0	1	1
Malaysia	0	0	1	1
Pakistan	0	0	1	1
Philippines	0	0	1	1
Puerto Rico	0	0	1	1
Qatar	0	0	1	1
Suriname	0	0	1	1
Thailand	0	0	1	1

SPORTS – BARCELONA 1992

Events: 257 in 30 sports – Archery | Athletics | Badminton | Baseball | Basketball | Basque Pelota | Boxing | Canoeing | Cycling | Diving | Equestrian | Fencing | Football | Gymnastics | Handball | Hockey | Judo | Modern pentathlon | Rowing | Sailing | Shooting | Swimming | Synchronized swimming | Table tennis | Taekwondo | Tennis | Volleyball | Water polo | Weightlifting | Wrestling.

CHAPTER 14

1996: Atlanta

19 July – 9 August

Games of the XXVI Olympiad

Countries participating: 197

Athletes participating:
10,318 (6,806 men, 3,512 women)

Events: 271 in 29 sports

Triple heavyweight champion Muhammad Ali, his movements slow and his hands shaking, defied the debilitating effects of Parkinson's disease to light the Olympic flame during the opening ceremony of the Atlanta Games. His determination and strength of will brought tears to the eyes of many of the spectators. Ali's return to the public stage after a decade out of the limelight was a moment of untarnished sporting spirit that launched a Games that was otherwise marked – and some say marred – by gross commercialisation.

The Olympics are, of course, a money-hungry circus but the 1996 events were the first staged without any governmental support, and this led to a mass-marketing exercise that critics claimed tarnished the traditional ideal of the Games. Thus the real winners were seen to be not the athletes, but the ad-men and marketeers who paid megabucks to put their Olympic trademarks on everything from T-shirts to seat cushions.

Companies including Reebok, Visa, Xerox and Atlanta-based Coca-Cola had paid an estimated \$800million for their branding. So, long before the Games were opened by President Bill Clinton, the IOC organised a team of lawyers and licensing agents to target trademark violators. A 250-man task force was even in evidence during the course of the events, checking on illicit souvenir sellers impertinent enough to sneak into the grounds.

The aura of unsubtle commercialism was hardly what the city of Atlanta had set out to achieve. Former mayor Andrew Young, who was instrumental in securing the Games for his town, boasted: "We want to be for the world what London was in the seventeenth and eighteenth centuries." The city fathers talked up their town as 'capital of the twentieth century' and 'hi-tech metropolis of the future'.

In fact, the city's bid had been a long-shot, particularly as the US had played host only twelve years earlier in Los Angeles. Known as the 'Centennial Games', the 1996 Olympics had strong rival contenders: Manchester, Melbourne, Belgrade, favourite Toronto and Athens, which wanted to mark the 100th anniversary of the first modern Games in Greece in 1896.

So it was sad that, Atlanta having won the bidding, many critics felt that the organisation of the Games left a lot to be desired.

Ironically what seemed to spur an Olympic spirit in both organisers and the public was a bomb blast at the crowded Centennial Olympic Park on 27 July. Flying shrapnel killed spectator Alice Hawthorne and wounded 111 others. It also caused the death of Turkish journalist Melih Uzunyol, who suffered a heart attack while hurrying to cover the explosion. The suspected perpetrator, Eric Robert Rudolph, was not caught until 2003 and was jailed for life for this and several other politically motivated bombings.

There was a determination not to allow a terror attack to derail the Games and within three days fans returned to the reopened Centennial Park, designed as 'town square' for the events. Records again began to fall and sporting heroes new and old were further crowned.

America's Carl Lewis and Michael Johnson were the supreme stars of the track – the latter clinching the unequalled achievement of winning both the 400 and 200 metres gold medals. Only four other men had even made the finals in both events. Johnson already held the world record in the 200 metres but took 0.34 of a second off that to finish in 19.32 seconds. As a consequence Johnson's popularity soared and he became the highest paid athlete in history, earning up to $100,000 an appearance.

Perhaps an even greater achievement at Atlanta was Carl Lewis's record ninth gold. Surprisingly for the man who had consistently long-jumped beyond 28 feet, Lewis had been on the verge of elimination in the preliminary round but managed to make a qualifying leap on his last attempt and went on to the final. He bowed out after Atlanta having won a fourth consecutive long jump, matching the record of American discus thrower Al Oerter, the first track and field performer to win four consecutive golds in one event

Then aged thirty-five and hailed as 'the greatest athlete in history', Lewis's career tally was nine Olympic golds, eight world championship golds and two world records. It tied him in gold medals with distance runner Paavo Nurmi of Finland, who won gold nine times between 1920 and 1928. Lewis is also credited with the greatest number of 100 metres run under 10 seconds.

Americans dominated the medal tables, sometimes despite severe adversity. Jackie Joyner-Kersee was forced to withdraw from the heptathlon because of leg injuries and asthma. Yet she returned a few days later for what became her most memorable Olympic performance. Struggling in the long jump, she slipped to sixth place before her final attempt. Then, in a tremendous display of willpower, she summoned the strength to make a leap that earned her a bronze medal.

Another heroine emerged among the young US gymnasts, who won the all-round team title and became labelled the 'Magnificent Seven'. Eighteen-year-old Kerri Strug was the hero of the hour when, her leg strapped heavily after an earlier injury, she put herself forward for a final vault. Obviously in pain she asked her coach Bela Karolyi: "Do we really need this?" The reply: "Kerri, we need you to go one more time, one more time for the gold. You can do it, you better do it." Strug limped forward, landed the vault on both feet, saluted the judges, then collapsed onto her knees in agony.

Other heroes and heroines emerged from among the near-10,000 athletes, representing 197 countries, including new entrants Hong Kong and the Palestinian Authority. France's Marie-Jose Perec equalled Michael Johnson's feat by winning the women's 200 and 400 metres events. Josiah Thugwane became the first black South African to strike gold in the marathon. And Ethiopia's smiling Fatuma Roba appeared tireless as she entered the Olympic Stadium to gain gold in the women's event.

Hungary's Krisztina Egerszegi became the first swimmer in history to win five individual Olympic gold medals. By surging past rivals in the 200 metres backstroke, the seventeen-year-old also became the only swimmer besides Australia's Dawn Fraser to win the same event in three different Olympics. "I like all the gold medals, but the last one is the best," she said. As further evidence of her sporting nature, Egerszegi had passed up a chance to swim the 100 metres backstroke to be on a relay team with her fellow Hungarians.

Russia's Svetlana Masterkova, a twenty-eight-year-old mother who had taken a two-year break from middle-distance running to marry and start a family, took golds in the 800 metres and 1,500 metres. After the 800, a Russian fan cried: "Do it again, Svetlana." The cheerful champion obliged by sprinting up both straights for the fastest lap of honour in history.

The Georgia Tech Aquatic Centre, Atlanta, was the scene of controversial triumphs for Irish swimmer Michelle Smith. Within the first five days of events the twenty-eight-year-old emerged from obscurity to claim three gold medals. She also won a bronze. But because of her unrated background the rumours began that she had used performance-enhancing drugs.

The allegations were boosted by the presence of her Dutch husband and coach, Erik De Bruin, a former discus thrower who had been given a four-year ban following a positive drugs test. The president of the Irish Olympic Council accused critics of a witch hunt and even US President Clinton entered the debate, personally urging Smith (who entered under her maiden name at Atlanta) to ignore complaints by her swimming rivals.

Smith returned home to a heroic welcome. Two years later, however, she received a four-year ban after being found guilty of attempting to cover up the fact that she had taken anabolic steroids. The International Swimming Federation said she used alcohol to tamper with urine samples taken in January 1998.

Britain's hero of the Games was Steve Redgrave, who triumphed in the coxless pairs to become only the fourth person in the modern Games to win four gold medals over four consecutive Olympiads. At the age of thirty-four, the determined veteran and his partner Matthew Pinsent set an early lead but lost pace – and the Australian pair of David Weightman and Robert Scott closed to within a second by the race's end. Acknowledging the narrowness of their win, the exhausted Redgrave said: "If anyone finds me close to a rowing boat again, they can shoot me." However, four years later, he was back aboard in Sydney, competing for an unprecedented fifth gold.

A less successful British veteran was thirty-six-year-old sprinter Linford Christie. In 1993 he had become the first man in history to hold the Olympic, World, European and Commonwealth titles in the 100 metres. He was also voted BBC Sports Personality of the Year. But at Atlanta he was dethroned as Olympic champion in sensational fashion. Christie made two false starts in the 100 metres final, encouraging media critics to suggest that he was avoiding the ignominy of defeat. Ultimately, he did cross the finish line – but long after Canadian Donovan Bailey had claimed the gold with a record time of 9.84 seconds, achieved by running at up to 27.07 mph, the fastest ever recorded.

It was not the greatest swansong for a British champion. Neither, on 9 August, was it the greatest ending of the most commercialised Olympics in history. In his closing speech IOC president Juan Antonio Samaranch described the Games as "most exceptional" and added: "Well done, Atlanta." He failed to praise them as "the best Olympics ever" – a significant break with tradition and a practice he would resume four years later in Sydney.

MEDALS TABLE
ATLANTA 1996 – GAMES OF THE XXVI OLYMPIAD
SUMMER OLYMPIC GAMES

Nation	Gold	Silver	Bronze	Total
United States	44	32	25	101
Russia	26	21	16	63
Germany	20	18	27	65
China	16	22	12	50
France	15	7	15	37
Italy	13	10	12	35
Australia	9	9	23	41
Cuba	9	8	8	25
Ukraine	9	2	12	23
South Korea	7	15	5	27
Poland	7	5	5	17
Hungary	7	4	10	21
Spain	5	6	6	17
Romania	4	7	9	20
Netherlands	4	5	10	19
Greece	4	4	0	8
Czech Republic	4	3	4	11
Switzerland	4	3	0	7
Denmark	4	1	1	6
Turkey	4	1	1	6
Canada	3	11	8	22
Bulgaria	3	7	5	15
Japan	3	6	5	14
Kazakhstan	3	4	4	11
Brazil	3	3	9	15
New Zealand	3	2	1	6
South Africa	3	1	1	5
Ireland	3	0	1	4
Sweden	2	4	2	8
Norway	2	2	3	7
Belgium	2	2	2	6
Nigeria	2	1	3	6
North Korea	2	1	2	5

1996: ATLANTA

Nation	Gold	Silver	Bronze	Total
Algeria	2	0	1	3
Ethiopia	2	0	1	3
Great Britain	1	8	6	15
Belarus	1	6	8	15
Kenya	1	4	3	8
Jamaica	1	3	2	6
Finland	1	2	1	4
Indonesia	1	1	2	4
Yugoslavia	1	1	2	4
Iran	1	1	1	3
Slovakia	1	1	1	3
Armenia	1	1	0	2
Croatia	1	1	0	2
Portugal	1	0	1	2
Thailand	1	0	1	2
Burundi	1	0	0	1
Costa Rica	1	0	0	1
Ecuador	1	0	0	1
Hong Kong	1	0	0	1
Syria	1	0	0	1
Argentina	0	2	1	3
Namibia	0	2	0	2
Slovenia	0	2	0	2
Austria	0	1	2	3
Malaysia	0	1	1	2
Moldova	0	1	1	2
Uzbekistan	0	1	1	2
Azerbaijan	0	1	0	1
Bahamas	0	1	0	1
Chinese Taipei	0	1	0	1
Latvia	0	1	0	1
Philippines	0	1	0	1
Tonga	0	1	0	1
Zambia	0	1	0	1
Georgia	0	0	2	2
Morocco	0	0	2	2
Trinidad and Tobago	0	0	2	2
India	0	0	1	1

Nation	Gold	Silver	Bronze	Total
Israel	0	0	1	1
Lithuania	0	0	1	1
Mexico	0	0	1	1
Mongolia	0	0	1	1
Mozambique	0	0	1	1
Puerto Rico	0	0	1	1
Tunisia	0	0	1	1
Uganda	0	0	1	1

SPORTS – ATLANTA 1996

Events: 271 in 29 sports – Archery | Athletics | Badminton | Baseball | Basketball | Boxing | Canoeing | Cycling | Diving | Equestrian | Fencing | Football | Gymnastics | Handball | Hockey | Judo | Modern pentathlon | Rowing | Sailing | Shooting | Softball | Swimming | Synchronized swimming | Table tennis | Tennis | Volleyball | Water polo | Weightlifting | Wrestling.

CHAPTER 15

2000: Sydney

15 September – 1 October

Games of the XXVII Olympiad

Countries participating: 199

Athletes participating:
10,651 (6,582 men, 4,069 women)

Events: 300 in 31 sports

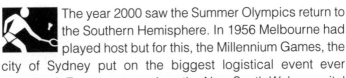 The year 2000 saw the Summer Olympics return to the Southern Hemisphere. In 1956 Melbourne had played host but for this, the Millennium Games, the city of Sydney put on the biggest logistical event ever organised. For seventeen days the New South Wales capital became the stage for one big party, providing the world with some of the greatest sporting events ever witnessed in the history of the modern Olympics.

With a record 199 nations (plus four individual athletes) participating, these Games were to see the tumbling of numerous world records. Australian author Bill Bryson best summed it up when he later wrote: "I don't wish in my giddiness to overstate matters, but I invite you to suggest a more successful event anywhere in the peacetime history of humankind. Certainly I know of no other occasion when so many people were so continuously cheerful."

Sydney began preparing for the Olympics in 1993 after being selected over Beijing, Berlin, Istanbul and Manchester in four rounds of IOC voting. Unlike Beijing (2008), Sydney sold out all its events. And unlike Athens (2004), their venue constructions had been fully completed.

The cost of playing host was astronomical: A$6.6 billion. But the infrastructure of the city of Sydney was to benefit enormously from the revamp. The suburb of Homebush Bay in western Sydney was redeveloped to house the Olympic Park, which provided venues for fourteen of the twenty-eight sports and the main stadium of the Games. Then labelled Stadium Australia and now known as ANZ Stadium, the A$690 million structure, with a seating capacity of 110,000, opened on 6 March 1999, just two-and-a-half years after builders first broke ground. The arena was home for many of the showpiece events, including track and field.

Darling Harbour, on the edge of Sydney Central Business District, became home to the convention centre with a capacity of 3,840, plus five exhibition halls seating between 5,000 and 10,000 people, staging the venues for the wrestling, judo, boxing, weightlifting and fencing events. There were a further eleven locations stretching across the Sydney district, from Penrith Lakes in the suburb of Cranebrook some 65 kilometres west of downtown Sydney, which hosted the rowing and canoeing/kayaking events, to a temporary arena built for beach volleyball on famous Bondi Beach, the first time the event had been held next to the sea.

The Opening Ceremony of the Games saw an ecstatic crowd cheer the entrance of a lone rider, Steve Jefferys, who galloped into Stadium Australia on his stock horse Ammo. He was swiftly followed, at the crack of his whip, by a further 120 riders, their stock horses performing intricate movements including a formation of the five Olympic rings. The theme throughout the ceremony was a celebration of the Australian continent and its pastoral heritage.

Entering the arena for The Parade of Nations were a record 199 countries. Andrew Gaze, basketball captain and five times Olympian, had the privilege of leading out the largest ever Australian team of 632 athletes. In an unusual display of unity, North and South Korea, although competing separately, marched together under the same flag. Four individual athletes from East Timor, not recognised as an independent country, were allowed to parade behind the IOC flag. The only significant nation absent in 2000 was Afghanistan, suspended by the IOC due to the Taliban regime's ban on most sports and its discrimination against women.

The Governor General of Australia Sir William Deane, officially opened the Games and Rechelle Hawkes (hockey) and Peter Kerr (water polo) took the Olympic and official oath. A marching band of 2,000 musicians (1,000 from Australia, the remaining from the rest of the world), requiring six conductors, held the crowd in awe, as did Olivia Newton-John and John Farnham who sang the duet 'Dare to Dream' as they walked among the athletes. To recognise a century of women's participation in the Olympics the torch was carried around the stadium by former Australian women Olympic champions: Betty Cuthbert, Raelene Boyle, Dawn Fraser, Shirley Strickland de la Hunty, Shane Gould and Debbie Flintoff-King. The torch was finally handed over to Cathy Freeman, the Aboriginal 400 metres world champion, who lit the flame in the cauldron within a circle of fire. Due to an electrical hitch the cauldron was left suspended in mid-air for four minutes before it could continue its journey up a water covered ramp to the top of the stadium.

There were some truly great and happy moments and some sad and unusual ones during the two-week sporting tournament...

Eric 'the Eel' Moussambani, a twenty-one-year-old from Equatorial Guinea, won the hearts of millions worldwide when he set the slowest-ever time for a 100 metres swim, taking 112.72 seconds – and sadly, as a result, was banned from training in his country's only swimming pool. Unlike the rest of the world his countrymen felt he had embarrassed their nation. He said later: "People have been downright rude to me. Some say I have brought shame on my country. When I got off the plane the only people to meet me at the airport were my parents. And what's worse is that I now have to train in the sea because the manager of the hotel which has the only swimming pool in Equatorial Guinea has told me I'm no longer welcome."

Another sad moment was on Day fourteen when the death of former Canadian Prime Minister Pierre Trudeau was announced. Canada was permitted to fly its flag at half-mast for the remainder of the Games.

The most successful athlete at the Sydney Games was Australian swimmer Ian Thorpe, known also as 'Thorpedo' or 'Thorpey', who specialised in freestyle but also competed in backstroke and the individual medley. Great things were expected of him, having previously broken the 200 metres freestyle world record in the 1999 World Championships and the 400 metres freestyle record in the 1999 Pan Pacific Championships. In the International Aquatic Centre the seventeen-year-old did not disappoint his fans, breaking his own world record in the 400 metres freestyle with a time of 3 minutes 40.59 seconds and gaining two further golds and world records in the 4 x 100 metres freestyle relay and 4 x 200 metres freestyle relay. He also won silver medals in the 200 metres freestyle and 4 x 100 metres medley relay. Former Australian head coach Don Talbot labelled him as "the greatest swimmer the world has seen".

Thorpe's success prompted allegations that he had used banned performance-enhancing steroids. There was an unpleasant confrontation before the start of the Games when the head coach and captain of Germany's swimming team accused him of cheating. According to the Germans Thorpe's physical attributes were symptomatic of steroid use and his ability to exceed prior records was drug-fuelled. The allegations were wholly unproven. Yet drug enforcement was taken very seriously at Sydney. It was the first time the Games saw The EPO (Erthropoietin, a peptide hormone that is produced naturally by the human body) detection test being used, as well as the presence of WADA (World Anti-Doping Agency), an independent body monitoring all the procedures followed by the IOC.

A proven drugs scandal that really shook the sporting world followed the fantastic success of American sprinter Marion Jones, dubbed 'the fastest woman on earth', who made history on the Sydney track by claiming five medals. Jones landed three gold medals, winning the 100 metres dash, the 200 metres dash and the 1,600 metres relay, adding two bronze medals in the long jump and the 400 metres relay.

Seven years later she lost her reputation and her five medals after admitting taking steroids before the 2000 Games. She also forfeited all other medals and prizes dating back to that year for her false denials of drug use to the press, sports agencies and two grand juries that had investigated the subject. Jones was also landed with a six-month jail sentence.

Back in 2000, Jones, then aged twenty-four, had been America's golden girl, standing alongside fellow countryman Michael Johnson, thirty-three, likewise dubbed 'the fastest man on earth'. Johnson's reputation, following his successes at Atlanta, remained unsullied. For in Sydney the 400 metres world record champion struck gold again, making him the only man to win the 400 metres in two consecutive Olympic Games. That brought his total number of Olympic golds to four. It could have been higher but for an injury he sustained in the 200 metres final, thereby preventing the defence of his hard-won Atlanta title.

Among the British contingent there was hard-fought success for thirty-year-old ex-soldier Kelly Holmes, who won her first Olympic medal:

bronze in the 800 metres. It was a foundation that the injury-plagued Holmes would build upon four years later in Athens.

Team GB totted up a creditable number of gold medals, however. There was an early success at the Sydney Olympic Shooting Centre where Richard Faulds came top with a sensational performance in the men's double trap shoot-out, beating Australia's Russell Mark.

On the track and field GB's Jonathan Edwards took Britain's gold medal tally to six with a world record of 18.29 metres in the triple jump, overcoming his disappointment at Atlanta where, going in as favourite and world record holder, he had managed only silver with a jump of 17.88 metres.

But it was off the track that Team GB excelled. The converted sand and gravel quarry at Penrith Lakes, one of the most beautiful venues of the Games, saw some spectacular personal feats, in particular for Great Britain's Steve Redgrave. Having won gold in the four previous Olympics (Coxed Four in 1984, Coxless Pair 1988, Coxless Pair 1992 and Coxless Pair 1996), he was going for an unprecedented fifth – the toughest challenge of all. In the Coxless Four race with Matthew Pinsent, James Cracknel and Tim Foster, the Britons crossed the finishing line 0.38 seconds ahead of the Italian crew. It was a micro moment between success and failure – and the revenge Redgrave was seeking after their defeat in Lucerene a few months earlier by the mighty Italians: Carlo Mornati, Valter Molea, Riccardo Dei Rossi and Lorenzo Carboncini.

Media pundits recalled Redgrave's self-effacing quote after his 1996 Atlanta win – "If anyone finds me close to a rowing boat again, they can shoot me" – yet in Sydney, battling with the limitations of ulcerative colitis and diabetes, he achieved the seemingly impossible, universally lauded as only the fourth Olympian to have won gold medals at five consecutive Games. He was made an MBE in 1987, a CBE in 1997 and he became a Knight Bachelor in 2001. In 2002 his Olympic Golds were voted Number One in Channel 4 TV's '100 Greatest Sporting Moments'.

Claiming another Team GB gold was a further success story at Penrith in the men's Coxed Eights. The squad of Andrew Lindsay, Ben Hunt-Davies, Simon Dennis, Louis Attrill, Luka Grubor, Kieran West, Fred Scarlett, Steve Trapmore and cox Rowley-Douglas led from start to finish, although arch-rivals Australia launched a late charge from the lane next to them. Britain held firm to win in a time of 5 minutes 33.08 seconds, a 0.8 margin over the host nation, with Croatia forced to settle for bronze. It was Britain's first gold medal in the men's eight since 1912.

There were some happy moments for Team GB's sailors at the picturesque harbour of Rushcutters Bay. Against the glorious backdrop of Sydney Harbour Bridge, Shirley Robertson, thirty-two, had a thrilling finish to win gold in the women's Europe class and twenty-three-year-old Ben Ainslee won gold in the laser dinghy class. Further medals were won by Iain Percy, who took gold in the single-handed Finn class, and Ian Walker and Mark Covell, who won silver in the Star keelboat, rounding off an almost perfect Olympic regatta.

There were some additions to the sporting agenda in 2000: the Triathlon and the martial art of Taekwondo, in which Vietnam won its first Olympic medal since it began competing in 1952, with Hieu Ngan taking silver in the women's 49-57 kg category. There were further firsts with women partaking in the modern pentathlon and weightlifting.

The men's football final had the Olympic Stadium spellbound. In a David and Goliath contest, Cameroon beat Spain to a historic gold medal in a nail-biting game that went to a penalty shoot-out, which Cameroon won 5-3.

The final event of the Games was the men's marathon, won by Ethiopian Genzhnge Abera, echoing that nation's success in the event in the 1960s when Abebe Bikila and Mamo Wolde became national heroes for their gold medals at Rome, Tokyo and Mexico City.

At the closing ceremony on 1 October – the day that Sydneysiders labelled 'Sad Sunday' because of the closure of such a festive event – the IOC's president Juan Antonio Samaranch declared: "I am proud and happy to proclaim that you have presented to the world the best Olympic Games ever." No-one could argue with that. The Games of the XXVII Olympiad will go down as one of the greatest ever in terms of the setting, organisation, hospitality and action. As the fireworks exploded across Sydney Harbour, the proud Australian hosts knew they had set a very high benchmark for how future Olympics should be staged.

2000: SYDNEY

MEDALS TABLE
SYDNEY 2000 – GAMES OF THE XXVII OLYMPIAD
SUMMER OLYMPIC GAMES

Nation	Gold	Silver	Bronze	Total
United States	39	25	33	97
Russia	32	28	28	88
China	28	16	15	59
Australia	16	25	17	58
Germany	13	17	26	56
France	13	14	11	38
Italy	13	8	13	34
Netherlands	12	9	4	25
Cuba	11	11	7	29
Great Britain	11	10	7	28
Romania	11	6	9	26
South Korea	8	10	10	28
Hungary	8	6	3	17
Poland	6	5	3	14
Japan	5	8	5	18
Bulgaria	5	6	2	13
Greece	4	6	3	13
Sweden	4	5	3	12
Norway	4	3	3	10
Ethiopia	4	1	3	8
Ukraine	3	10	10	23
Kazakhstan	3	4	0	7
Belarus	3	3	11	17
Canada	3	3	8	14
Spain	3	3	5	11
Turkey	3	0	2	5
Iran	3	0	1	4
Czech Republic	2	3	3	8
Kenya	2	3	2	7
Denmark	2	3	1	6
Finland	2	1	1	4
Austria	2	1	0	3
Lithuania	2	0	3	5

Nation	Gold	Silver	Bronze	Total
Azerbaijan	2	0	1	3
Slovenia	2	0	0	2
Switzerland	1	6	2	9
Indonesia	1	3	2	6
Slovakia	1	3	1	5
Mexico	1	2	3	6
Algeria	1	1	3	5
Uzbekistan	1	1	2	4
Latvia	1	1	1	3
Yugoslavia	1	1	1	3
Bahamas	1	1	0	2
New Zealand	1	0	3	4
Estonia	1	0	2	3
Thailand	1	0	2	3
Croatia	1	0	1	2
Cameroon	1	0	0	1
Colombia	1	0	0	1
Mozambique	1	0	0	1
Brazil	0	6	6	12
Jamaica	0	4	3	7
Nigeria	0	3	0	3
Belgium	0	2	3	5
South Africa	0	2	3	5
Argentina	0	2	2	4
Chinese Taipei	0	1	4	5
Morocco	0	1	4	5
North Korea	0	1	3	4
Moldova	0	1	1	2
Saudi Arabia	0	1	1	2
Trinidad and Tobago	0	1	1	2
Ireland	0	1	0	1
Uruguay	0	1	0	1
Vietnam	0	1	0	1
Georgia	0	0	6	6
Costa Rica	0	0	2	2
Portugal	0	0	2	2
Armenia	0	0	1	1
Barbados	0	0	1	1

2000: SYDNEY

Nation	Gold	Silver	Bronze	Total
Chile	0	0	1	1
Iceland	0	0	1	1
India	0	0	1	1
Israel	0	0	1	1
Kuwait	0	0	1	1
Kyrgyzstan	0	0	1	1
FYR Macedonia	0	0	1	1
Qatar	0	0	1	1
Sri Lanka	0	0	1	1

SPORTS – SYDNEY 2000

Events: 300 in 31 sports – Archery | Athletics | Badminton | Baseball | Basketball | Boxing | Canoeing | Cycling | Diving | Equestrian | Fencing | Football (soccer) | Gymnastics | Handball | Hockey | Judo | Modern pentathlon | Rowing | Sailing | Shooting | Softball | Swimming | Synchronized swimming | Table tennis | Taekwondo | Tennis | Triathlon | Volleyball | Water polo | Weightlifting | Wrestling.

CHAPTER **16**

2004: Athens

13 August – 29 August

Games of the XXVIII Olympiad

Countries participating: 201

Athletes participating:
10,625 (6,296 men, 4,329 women)

Events: 301 in 31 sports

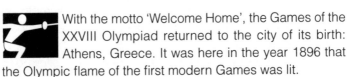 With the motto 'Welcome Home', the Games of the XXVIII Olympiad returned to the city of its birth: Athens, Greece. It was here in the year 1896 that the Olympic flame of the first modern Games was lit.

But how these modern Olympic Games have grown... In 1896 fewer than 1,000 athletes (975 men, only 22 women) from fourteen nations competed in forty-three events in nine sports. From this modest nine-day tournament has evolved the present century's two-week spectacular, way beyond the hopes and dreams of many, including the founder of the modern Games, Pierre de Coubertin.

Although lobbied by dignitaries like Greece's King George for the Olympics to be held continually in Athens, it took more than a century for the Games to return to Greece, the country easily defeating rival Rome in the 1997 IOC bidding to be nominated host for the XXVIII Olympiad.

Once the choice had been made, Greece launched itself on a massive building project using new and old venues from four different centuries. The main Olympic Sports Complex was spread out across suburban Marousi, north-east of Athens. Other venues were located in Volos, 300 kilometres to the north of the capital, Patras, 200 kilometres to the west, Thessaloniki in Macedonia, Heraklion on the island of Crete and Ancient Olympia itself.

The heart of the Games was the Olympic stadium within the Sports Complex. Named after the first modern marathon race winner in 1896, the 'Spiros Louis Stadium' hosted the opening and closing ceremonies, the athletics and the finals of the football. With time fast running out to finish its construction, 700 volunteers were needed to bring this massive project to completion. The stadium's 16,000 ton glass and steel dome, designed by the Spanish architect Santiago Calatrava, caused the biggest worry and was finished just in time for the opening ceremony. However, the roof over the Aquatic center had to be aborted, which meant all swimming events took place outside, the first time since Barcelona in 1992.

Greece's transport system needed updating if it was to meet the demands of a modern Olympics. These major works were also lagging desperately but by early August the new light railway linking the capital to its coastal communities along the Saronic Gulf was up and running, as were an upgraded Athens ring road and its Metro system.

On 13 August, 72,000 spectators filled the Olympic Stadium. To achieve their theme of uniting old with new the centre of the venue had been transformed into a lake upon which a little boy on a paper boat and carrying a Greek flag opened the celebrations, followed by centaurs and Greek gods and a spectacular pyrotechnic display stretching across the huge arch that towered over the stadium. A parade of 10,500 athletes then entered the stadium arranged in Greek alphabetical order. Significantly, after previous Games boycotts, Athens 2004 was the first since 1996 in which all countries with a National Olympic Committee were in attendance.

A shadow had been cast over the Games, however, even before they got under way. Performance enhancing drugs were the particular blight of the Athens Olympics.

Two Greek athletes, Kostas Kenteris, the 200 metres gold medalist at Sydney in 2000, and Katerina Thanou, the women's 100 metres silver medalist, withdrew from the Games having missed a drugs test. Their claim that they had both been in a motorcycle crash and therefore unable to make the test was later found to be untrue.

It was not an isolated case. In all, by the time the flame was distinguished at the end of the Games, twenty-four athletes had tested positive to performance enhancing drugs, doubling the highest previous number of twelve at Los Angeles in 1984. Russian Irina Korzhanenko had her gold medal in the shot put expropriated as did Hungary's Robert Fazekas in the discus and Adrian Annus in the hammer

The media labelled it the "dirtiest Games ever". But with over 3,000 tests carried out, a twenty-five per cent increase on the number conducted in Sydney, IOC president Jacques Rogge knew these would produce more positive results than ever before. Rogge argued that, rather than contaminating the Olympic ideal, these Games had actually benefited by the exposure of more drug cheats. He said: "You have 10,500 athletes in the Olympic village – you do not have 10,500 saints. What counts is that we act against this evil drug use. Every positive test catches a cheat and protects a clean athlete."

An even greater headache than drugs was security. The 11 September 2001 atrocity in New York, followed by Al Qaeda attacks in Europe, heightened the Greek government's awareness of the potential for terrorism and unprecedented measures were put in place to defeat it. In 2004 the threat of a nuclear dirty bomb attack was considered very real.

A record one billion Euros had been earmarked for the Games security budget – three times higher than for Sydney four years earlier – and 70,000 armed personnel, police, coastguards and emergency servicemen had been allocated to protect the Olympics. An 'air defence umbrella' of Mirage 2000 and F-16 interception fighter jets, backed by Patriot, Stinger and Hawk missile batteries, protected Athens and the other venues throughout the Games.

This did not wholly reassure some Americans, including Munich swim hero Mark Spitz who suggested the US team might well withdraw from the Games. The British Olympic Association thought otherwise, stating: "We are very confident and comfortable with the security provisions outlined." Their point was proved when a Greek National Intelligence Service and a foreign Intelligence Service operation successfully uncovered a large amount of explosives.

The problems surrounding drugs and security highlighted the contrast between the ancient and the modern Games. But there were more positive links. The Panathenaic Stadium which had been a venue during the 1896 Olympics was back in use – and had an even older connection, the Panathenaic Games having been held every four years in Athens from 566 BC through to the third century AD. In 2004 the Panathenaic Stadium was used for the archery competitions and housed the Media Centres. From here was relayed the first-ever international broadcast of high-definition television, helping make this the most watched Olympics in history.

In this same Panathenaic Stadium 45,000 people gathered to see the final of the marathon that followed the same route as the 1896 race. It was in this event that one of the strangest moments of the Games occurred. Italy's Stefano Baldini took gold but his victory was overshadowed after one of the runners was attacked by a bystander. Brazilian Vanderlei de Lima was leading when the seemingly deranged protestor, an Irish ex-priest, pushed him to the side of the road four miles from the finish. He recovered to win a bronze, saying: "If it were not for that lunatic, I would have won the gold. I was unstoppable."

De Lima and the Brazilian Olympic Committee appealed in vain to the International Amateur Athletics Federation and the Court for Arbitration in Sport for a duplicate gold to be awarded to the Brazilian. The CAS said it "had no power to remedy his legitimate frustration". However a consolation prize for de Lima was awarded at the closing ceremony. The IOC presented him with a medal named after the founder of the modern Games, Pierre De Coubertin, "in recognition of his exceptional demonstration of fair play and Olympic values".

One man took an unusually high share of medals. Michael Phelps, the US swimmer, became the first athlete to win eight medals: six gold and two bronze. Although he made his big splash in 2004, Phelps had been notable in 2000 as the youngest male on the US team in Sydney, where he had finished fifth in the 200 metres butterfly. In Athens, his extraordinary physique won him greater glory. His six-foot four-inch frame looked as if it was built for speed – with an arm-span of six foot seven inches powering him along, an extra-long torso allowing him to stay high on the water, and size-14 feet giving him a powerful kick.

Phelps's golden tally was: 100 metres butterfly, 200 metres butterfly, 200 metres individual medley, 400 metres individual medley, 4 x 100 metres medley relay and 4 x 200 metres freestyle relay. The bronze were for: 4 x 100 metres freestyle relay and 200 metres freestyle. His achievement was just one gold medal short of matching the record seven golds Mark Spitz earned in 1972.

There were other notable firsts in 2004... The US lost for the first time in men's basketball since NBA players were admitted, defeated by

Puerto Rico 92-73. Israel got its first gold medal, thanks to windsurfer Gal Fridman. The Dominican Republic got its first gold when Felix Sanchez won the 400 metres hurdles. China got its first gold in track and field when Liu Xiang won the 110 metres hurdles, equalling Colin Jackson's 1993 world record of 12.91 seconds.

A unique record was set by German kayaker Birgit Fischer who won the K-4 500 metres and came second in the K-2 500 metres. She thereby became the first woman in any sport to win gold medals at six different Olympics – stretching from first to last, twenty-four years apart.

Morocco's Hicham El Guerrouj crowned his illustrious career by winning both the 1,500 and 5,000 metres, the first person to do so since Finland's Paavo Nurmi in 1924. El Guerrouj later announced his retirement from athletics while holding three world records: the Mile (3:43.13), 2,000 metres (4:44.79) and 1,500 metres (3:26.00). El Guerrouj had been unbeaten in eighty-four out of eighty-nine competitions at the 1,500 metres since 1986.

For British spectators and television viewers, perhaps the saddest sight of the entire Games came when world record holder and strong favourie Paula Radcliffe, a Commonwealth, European and world champion, dropped out of the marathon. It was an upsetting image to see her sitting on the kerbside at the twenty-three-mile mark in obvious distress, suffering from the blazing heat and humidity of Athens.

The disappointment was made up for elsewhere. As in Sydney, there was joy for the British cycling, rowing and sailing teams. In the velodrome stadium the 5,000-seater cycling track saw Chris Hoy win Great Britain's second gold medal by clocking a new Olympic record to win the men's 1 kilometre cycling time trial. "I don't believe it," he said. "When I crossed the line, it didn't sink in for a few laps. I really didn't expect in a hundred years to go that fast."

Bradley Wiggins, after claiming a stunning cycling gold in the individual pursuit and silver in the team event, saved perhaps his finest ride until last to take bronze with Rob Hayles in the madison. Team GB signed off with two golds, a silver and a bronze, and Wiggins played a part in three of them.

In the men's coxless four Matthew Pinsent won a historic fourth gold medal in the Schinias Rowing Centre when, along with Sydney champions James Cracknell, Ed Coode and Steve Williams, they beat the world champions Canada in a photo finish by 0.08 seconds. Pinsent had won his first gold with Steve Redgrave in 1992 and had never lost an Olympic race, also triumphing at Atlanta 1996 and Sydney 2000.

Team GB dominated the sailing regatta for the second straight Games, winning two gold medals, one silver and two bronze. Ben Ainslee won one of the golds in the Finn class and the women won the second in the Ynling race.

GB's athletic team managed just four medals in fifty-eight competitions, Kelly Holmes saving her teammates' blushes from outright defeat. Setting a new British record she won double gold in the 800 metres and the 500 metres, thereby being hailed as one of the greatest achievers in her country's Olympic history.

Jason Gardener, Darren Campbell, Marlon Devonish and Mark Lewis-Francis won gold in the men's 4 x 100 metre relay. They outran the USA, the pre-race favourites, in a thrilling contest with just one hundredth of a second to spare. The fourth medal to be won was a bronze for Georgina Harland in the modern pentathlon. With 49 seconds adrift and in fourteenth place, she overtook twelve competitors in the last event, producing a superb comeback in the 3,000 metres run.

The head of the British Olympic Association, Simon Clegg, at one stage lamented: "There were far too many athletes not getting through the first rounds and being eliminated in early heats." However, having set a target of six to nine golds with a total in excess of twenty-five, Clegg was delighted to exclaim, "Mission accomplished", as the British team's final tally reached thirty medals – its best performance of modern times.

On 29 August, with balloons falling from the skies over the Olympic Stadium, Athens bid farewell to the Games of the XXVIII Olympiad. A young Greek girl, Fotini Papaleonidopoulou, lit a symbolic lantern with the Olympic Flame and passed it on to other children before extinguishing the flame in the cauldron by blowing a puff of air. The Athens Games, it was generally concluded, had turned out to be more successful than most had imagined. IOC president Jacques Rogge called it "the unforgettable, dream Games".

MEDALS TABLE
ATHENS 2004 – GAMES OF THE XXVIII OLYMPIAD
SUMMER OLYMPIC GAMES

Nation	Gold	Silver	Bronze	Total
United States	36	39	27	102
China	32	17	14	63
Russia	27	27	38	92
Australia	17	16	16	49
Japan	16	9	12	37
Germany	13	16	20	49
France	11	9	13	33
Italy	10	11	11	32
South Korea	9	12	9	30
Great Britain	9	9	12	30
Cuba	9	7	11	27
Ukraine	9	5	9	23
Hungary	8	6	3	17
Romania	8	5	6	19
Greece	6	6	4	16
Brazil	5	2	3	10
Norway	5	0	1	6
Netherlands	4	9	9	22
Sweden	4	2	1	7
Spain	3	11	5	19
Canada	3	6	3	12
Turkey	3	3	4	10
Poland	3	2	5	10
New Zealand	3	2	0	5
Thailand	3	1	4	8
Belarus	2	6	7	15
Austria	2	4	1	7
Ethiopia	2	3	2	7
Iran	2	2	2	6
Slovakia	2	2	2	6
Chinese Taipei	2	2	1	5
Georgia	2	2	0	4
Bulgaria	2	1	9	12

A GUIDE TO THE OLYMPIC GAMES AND LONDON 2012

Nation	Gold	Silver	Bronze	Total
Jamaica	2	1	2	5
Uzbekistan	2	1	2	5
Morocco	2	1	0	3
Denmark	2	0	6	8
Argentina	2	0	4	6
Chile	2	0	1	3
Kazakhstan	1	4	3	8
Kenya	1	4	2	7
Czech Republic	1	3	4	8
South Africa	1	3	2	6
Croatia	1	2	2	5
Lithuania	1	2	0	3
Egypt	1	1	3	5
Switzerland	1	1	3	5
Indonesia	1	1	2	4
Zimbabwe	1	1	1	3
Azerbaijan	1	0	4	5
Belgium	1	0	2	3
Bahamas	1	0	1	2
Israel	1	0	1	2
Cameroon	1	0	0	1
Dominican Republic	1	0	0	1
United Arab Emirates	1	0	0	1
North Korea	0	4	1	5
Latvia	0	4	0	4
Mexico	0	3	1	4
Portugal	0	2	1	3
Finland	0	2	0	2
Serbia and Montenegro	0	2	0	2
Slovenia	0	1	3	4
Estonia	0	1	2	3
Hong Kong	0	1	0	1
India	0	1	0	1
Paraguay	0	1	0	1
Colombia	0	0	2	2
Nigeria	0	0	2	2
Venezuela	0	0	2	2
Eritrea	0	0	1	1

2004: ATHENS

Nation	Gold	Silver	Bronze	Total
Mongolia	0	0	1	1
Syria	0	0	1	1
Trinidad and Tobago	0	0	1	1

SPORTS – ATHENS 2004

Events: 301 in 31 sports – Archery | Athletics | Badminton | Baseball | Basketball | Boxing | Canoeing | Cycling | Diving | Equestrian | Fencing | Football (soccer) | Gymnastics | Handball | Hockey | Judo | Modern pentathlon | Rowing | Sailing | Shooting | Softball | Swimming | Synchronized swimming | Table tennis | Taekwondo | Tennis | Triathlon | Volleyball | Water polo | Weightlifting | Wrestling.

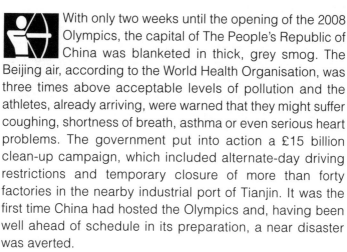

CHAPTER **17**

2008: Beijing

8 August – 24 August

Games of the XXIX Olympiad

Countries participating: 204

Athletes participating:
11,196 (6,450 men, 4,746 women)

Events: 302 in 31 sports

With only two weeks until the opening of the 2008 Olympics, the capital of The People's Republic of China was blanketed in thick, grey smog. The Beijing air, according to the World Health Organisation, was three times above acceptable levels of pollution and the athletes, already arriving, were warned that they might suffer coughing, shortness of breath, asthma or even serious heart problems. The government put into action a £15 billion clean-up campaign, which included alternate-day driving restrictions and temporary closure of more than forty factories in the nearby industrial port of Tianjin. It was the first time China had hosted the Olympics and, having been well ahead of schedule in its preparation, a near disaster was averted.

It was widely accepted that China had outspent any other previous Olympic host – and witnessing the opening ceremony, there could be no doubt that this was true.

The Beijing National Stadium, better known as the 'Bird's Nest' for its pattern inspired by Chinese-style 'crazed pottery', had cost £300 million and was hailed as the finest arena in the world. With a floor area of 254,600 square metres and a seating capacity of 91,000, this centrepiece of the most expensive Olympics ever was built to last 100 years and withstand earthquakes up to a magnitude of eight on the Richter Scale. The circular shape of the stadium represented 'heaven', while the adjacent square form of the National Aquatics Centre, known as the 'Water Cube', represented the Chinese symbol of Earth.

Among the 91,000 spectators gathered in the National Stadium by 8pm on 8 August – eight being considered a lucky number associated with prosperity and confidence in Chinese culture – were more than a hundred sovereigns and heads of state, the largest gathering in Olympic history. President Hu Jinato opened the ceremony that lasted more than four hours and reportedly cost £70 million.

The crowds were treated to spectacular and spellbinding performances of colourful dance, singing and fireworks, all directed by Chinese film director Zhang Yimou, with the final ascent to the torch featuring Olympic gymnast Li Ling, who appeared to run through air around the membrane of the stadium. An estimated 15,000 performers representing fifty-six ethnic groups took part in this spectacle, culminating in a flurry of fireworks in red and orange, some projecting Olympic Rings, others smiley faces.

Over the following days spectators at the Bird's Nest, used for athletics and football, witnessed some special thrills… Usain Bolt, the twenty-two-year-old Jamaican sprinter, broke three world records and won three golds. Yelena Isinbayeva, the Russian pole-vaulter, became the darling of the crowds by clearing a height of 5.05 metres, winning the gold medal and claiming her twenty-fourth world record . And Christine Ohuruogu, the twenty-four-year-old sprinter from East London, triumphed in the 400 metres, winning Great Britain's fiftieth gold medal in Olympic athletics.

The newly built Water Cube saw further breathtaking sporting achievements. Emphasising the importance the Chinese felt for their Games to be environmentally friendly, this stadium was built to a water-saving design concept that was praised as a gigantic, green, architectural wonder. Here the British girl Rebecca Adlington won two gold medals, one in the 400 metres freestyle and the other in the 800 metres, which she utterly dominated and in which she set a new world record. It had been almost half a century since a British woman had won an Olympic swimming gold medal.

2008: BEIJING

The Water Cube spectators were also treated to record-breaking achievements by Michael Phelps, the 'Baltimore Bullet'. Following his successes in Athens four years previously, the American collected eight gold medals, becoming the most successful athlete of the 2008 Games. His list of honours ran, in chronological order, thus: 400 metres individual medley (world record of 4 minutes 3.84 seconds), 4 x 100 metres freestyle relay (world record of 3 minutes 8.24 seconds), 200 metres freestyle (world record of 1 minute 42.96 seconds), 200 metres butterfly (world record of 1 minute 52.03 seconds), 4 x 200 metres freestyle relay (world record of 6 minutes 58.56 seconds), 200 metres individual medley (world record of one minute 54.23 seconds), 100 metres butterfly (Olympic record of 50.58 seconds) and 4 x 100 metres medley relay (world record of 3 minutes 29.34 seconds).

There was a slight controversy before the final of his seventh gold medal in the 100 metres butterfly when Serbian-American swimmer Milorad Cavic suggested it would be beneficial if Phelps lost. "It'd be good for him if he loses. It would be good if historians talk about Michael Phelps winning seven gold medals and losing the eight to 'some guy'. I'd like to be that guy." This remark made Phelps even more determined, spurring him on to win in his record-breaking 50.58 seconds, edging out Cavic by 1/100 of a second.

The swimsuit donned by Phelps and several other contestants caused some debate. It was the first time the high-performance swimwear, the Speedo LZR Racer, had made its appearance – having been developed using the science of shark-skin.

The Shunyi Olympic Rowing-Canoeing Park, a new purpose-built venue, had its fair share of excitement too, with Great Britain heading the medal table with two gold, two silver and two bronze. Andy Hodge, Peter Reed, Steve Williams and Tom James produced a thrilling race in the coxless four when they summoned up a late surge three-quarters of a length down to beat the rival Australians. "I don't know where that last 250 metres came from," said Hodge. "I was in so much pain – I've never been in that pain in my entire life." It was Great Britain's third successive win in this event.

Also on the water but this time on the southern coastline of the Shandong Peninsular, with the storm-tossed Qingdao harbour and its unique blend of sea and mountains, was the newly built Qingdao International Sailing Centre. Here the British squad dominated. Ben Ainslie won his third gold medal in as many Games in the Finn Class and the Great Britain women's Yngling trio fended off a strong Dutch challenge to claim another of the four golds won, which saw them head the sailing medals table by the end of the Games.

Cycling, in another newly built venue, the Laoshan Velodrome with a seating capacity of 6,000, was also making headlines with the British team dominating. Chris Hoy won three golds in the sprint, the keirin and the team sprint. Bradley Wiggins won the 4,000 metres individual pursuit, becoming the first rider ever to successfully defend his Olympic title, and then went on to help defeat the opposition in the team pursuit event. The women were to do just as well with the Welsh rider Nicole Cooke winning Britain's first gold medal in an exciting road race, clocking in a time of 32 minutes 24 seconds.

One of the most amazing achievements of the whole Games came from Rebecca Romero, or 'Romero the Rider,' who won gold in the individual pursuit. In the Athens Games four years earlier she had won silver in the quad sculls – and it was only two years afterwards that she had first cycled round a track. She is the first British woman ever to compete in two different Olympic sports and to win medals in both. Only one other woman has ever achieved this, East Germany's Roswitha Krause, both of hers coming as part of a team: a handball silver in the Montreal Games of 1976 following a freestyle relay silver in the Mexico Games of 1968.

The only lowlight came on the BMX course. Nineteen-year-old Briton Shanaze Reade, who had not lost a BMX final for three years, was distraught after crashing on the final corner and seeing her medal chances disappear in a cloud of yellow dust.

The Games of the XXIX Olympiad concluded with twelve finals, including a new record in the men's marathon, set by Samuel Kamau Wansiru. The Kenyan's time of 2 hours 6:32 minutes beat the twenty-four-year-old's previous record of 2 hours 9:21 minutes, set by Portugal's Carlos Lopes in Los Angeles in 1984.

Zou Shiming won China's first Olympic boxing gold and by so doing won its fiftieth gold medal of the Games. Elsewhere, as expected, world champions Russia won the rhythmic gymnastics all-round gold medal, scoring 35.550 points, closely followed by China in silver position with 35.225. The USA won the final of the men's basketball, beating a determined Spanish team 118 points to 107 – and, in so doing, redeemed their wounded pride at missing the gold medal in Athens.

2008: BEIJING

The Beijing Games set one further record, with more than forty-two per cent female athletes, revealing an increasing growth within the last two decades. The final medal table put China on top with fifty-one gold medals, the USA second with thirty-six, Russia third with twenty-one and Great Britain fourth with nineteen.

So national pride and sporting passion were evident throughout the Beijing Games. The mystery, though, was: where were all the fans? With a supposed record sale of all 6.8 million tickets, the Chinese organisers were baffled to have to acknowledge towards the end of the first week that there were too many empty seats at the venues. Even the opulent Olympic Park itself was thin on spectators inside and tourists outside. One embarrassing US newspaper headline reported: "Beijing is all dressed up, but no-one is going."

On some days, half the eighteen venues failed to reach eighty per cent capacity. Record-breaker Michael Phelps won his third gold medal in the 200 metres freestyle in an arena with at least 500 empty seats, with further no-shows as he took his fourth gold in the 200 metres butterfly. The US softball team played to a stadium with seventy per cent of the seats empty.

Chinese officials, quizzed by the IOC, blamed the heat, humidity and rain showers. But observers suggested that more likely reasons were the strict visa restrictions and tight domestic security. In the end the Beijing authorities filled the empty seats and artificially boosted the atmosphere by bussing in teams of state-trained 'cheer squads', readily identifiable by their uniformly bright yellow T-shirts.

However, by the time the Games of the XXIX came to a close, the final glittering ceremony was played out to a packed National Stadium. The celebration began with an explosion of fireworks lighting the sky in a rainbow of colours, followed by a brilliant display of dancing and drumming. The thousands of athletes joined the party as 200 flag bearers led the way. The IOC president, Jacques Rogge, summed up the Chinese success story in his closing speech, saying: "We have come to the end of sixteen days which we will cherish forever. These were a truly exceptional Games."

He and the mayor of Beijing, Guo Jinlong, then handed the Olympic flag over to Boris Johnson, the London mayor – launching an eight-minute presentation by the UK organisers to offer a taste of the 2012 Games. The star of the show was a red London bus but other celebrities who raised cheers from the crowd were singer Leona Lewis who, along with former Led Zeppelin guitarist Jimmy Page, sung a rendition of 'Whole Lotta Love' and David Beckham, who kicked a ball into the crowd of athletes.

Against a background dominated by security problems, pollution worries and their human rights record, it was universally agreed that China had hosted the most spectacular and the best organised Games in history.

2008: BEIJING

MEDALS TABLE
BEIJING 2008 – GAMES OF THE XXIX OLYMPIAD
SUMMER OLYMPIC GAMES

Nation	Gold	Silver	Bronze	Total
China	51	21	28	100
United States	36	38	36	110
Russia	23	21	28	72
Great Britain	19	13	15	47
Germany	16	10	15	41
Australia	14	15	17	46
South Korea	13	10	8	31
Japan	9	6	10	25
Italy	8	10	10	28
France	7	16	17	40
Ukraine	7	5	15	27
Netherlands	7	5	4	16
Jamaica	6	3	2	11
Spain	5	10	3	18
Kenya	5	5	4	14
Belarus	4	5	10	19
Romania	4	1	3	8
Ethiopia	4	1	2	7
Canada	3	9	6	18
Poland	3	6	1	10
Hungary	3	5	2	10
Norway	3	5	2	10
Brazil	3	4	8	15
Czech Republic	3	3	0	6
Slovakia	3	2	1	6
New Zealand	3	1	5	9
Georgia	3	0	3	6
Cuba	2	11	11	24
Kazakhstan	2	4	7	13
Denmark	2	2	3	7
Mongolia	2	2	0	4
Thailand	2	2	0	4
North Korea	2	1	3	6

A GUIDE TO THE OLYMPIC GAMES AND LONDON 2012

Nation	Gold	Silver	Bronze	Total
Argentina	2	0	4	6
Switzerland	2	0	4	6
Mexico	2	0	1	3
Turkey	1	4	3	8
Zimbabwe	1	3	0	4
Azerbaijan	1	2	4	7
Uzbekistan	1	2	3	6
Slovenia	1	2	2	5
Bulgaria	1	1	3	5
Indonesia	1	1	3	5
Finland	1	1	2	4
Latvia	1	1	1	3
Belgium	1	1	0	2
Dominican Republic	1	1	0	2
Estonia	1	1	0	2
Portugal	1	1	0	2
India	1	0	2	3
Iran	1	0	1	2
Cameroon	1	0	0	1
Panama	1	0	0	1
Tunisia	1	0	0	1
Sweden	0	4	1	5
Croatia	0	2	3	5
Lithuania	0	2	3	5
Greece	0	2	2	4
Trinidad and Tobago	0	2	0	2
Nigeria	0	1	3	4
Austria	0	1	2	3
Ireland	0	1	2	3
Serbia	0	1	2	3
Algeria	0	1	1	2
Bahamas	0	1	1	2
Colombia	0	1	1	2
Kyrgyzstan	0	1	1	2
Morocco	0	1	1	2
Tajikistan	0	1	1	2
Chile	0	1	0	1

2008: BEIJING

Nation	Gold	Silver	Bronze	Total
Ecuador	0	1	0	1
Iceland	0	1	0	1
Malaysia	0	1	0	1
South Africa	0	1	0	1
Singapore	0	1	0	1
Sudan	0	1	0	1
Vietnam	0	1	0	1
Armenia	0	0	6	6
Chinese Taipei	0	0	4	4
Afghanistan	0	0	1	1
Egypt	0	0	1	1
Israel	0	0	1	1
Moldova	0	0	1	1
Mauritius	0	0	1	1
Togo	0	0	1	1
Venezuela	0	0	1	1

SPORTS – BEIJING 2008

Events: 302 in 31 sports – Archery | Athletics | Badminton | Baseball | Basketball | Boxing | Canoeing | Cycling | Diving | Equestrian | Fencing | Field hockey | Football (soccer) | Gymnastics | Handball | Judo | Modern pentathlon | Rowing | Sailing | Shooting | Softball | Swimming | Synchronised swimming | Table tennis | Taekwondo | Tennis | Triathlon | Volleyball | Water Polo | Weightlifting | Wrestling.

CHAPTER **18**

The Winter Olympics

 This book is principally concerned with the Summer Olympics, especially those from London 1948 to London 2012. The Winter Olympic Games, of course, have run in tandem with the summer events since 1924.

Although part of an Olympic tradition that goes back 3,000 years, the winter events had a shaky start. The introduction of the first official Winter Olympics in 1924 was the culmination of a protracted struggle. Nations in warmer climates feared that sports favouring snow, ice and a cold climate would give an unfair advantage to countries where such activities as skating and skiing were more regularly practised. On the other side of the argument, the Scandinavian nations, which should have been prime movers in instigating such a gathering, were fearful that Winter Olympics would threaten their own Nordic games, which had been held every four years since 1901.

The International Olympic Committee solved the problem by organising what they termed an 'International Sports Week' at Chamonix, France, in 1924. Scandinavian athletes won twenty-eight out of the forty-three medals – and suddenly those countries dropped their objections. The event was retrospectively named the First Winter Olympic Games.

From then the Games were held every four years until 1936 when they were interrupted by war. When London agreed to resume the Summer Olympics in 1948, the Winter Games were held that year in the Swiss resort of St Moritz. In 1992 the pattern changed when the IOC voted to schedule the Summer and Winter Games on separate four-year cycles in alternating even-numbered years. Thus the next Winter Games after France hosted them in1992 were in Norway in 1994.

There have been many moments of sporting glory at these winter venues over the years – but there have also been ruinously unpredictable weather, political protests, boycotts and much bickering...

As we've seen, the First Winter Olympic Games at **Chamonix** in **1924** came about after delicate diplomacy by the IOC. America's Charles Jewtraw won the distinction of earning the first Winter Games gold medal in the 500 metres speed skating. The Nordic nations dominated elsewhere with Norway's cross-country skier Thorleif Haug taking three golds and Finland's speed skater Clas Thunberg taking three golds, a silver and a bronze.

Weather problems hampered the **1928** events in **St Moritz**. Lack of snow forced the cancellation of the 10,000 metres speed skating contest, after which eighteen hours of rain led to the postponement of an entire day's events. That still left time for 'Flying Finn' Thunberg to add two more golds to his 1924 tally. Another remarkable performance was by Norway's Sonja Henie who won the figure skating gold at the age of just fifteen.

The **1932** Games in **Lake Placid**, USA, caused the host nation some embarrassment when forced to transport snow by truck from Canada. America was still in the grip of the Depression and only seventeen countries sent athletes. As a consequence, the US topped the medal table with six golds. Remarkable among them was Eddie Eagan, the light-heavyweight boxing gold medallist in 1920, who was a member of the four-man bob team in 1932 – thereby becoming the only athlete to win summer and winter golds.

The **1936** Winter Olympics were, like the Summer Games, held in Nazi Germany in the twin villages of **Garmisch-Partenkirchen**, Bavaria. They were deemed successful – despite being stained by the regime's propaganda exercise. Anti-Semitic posters and pamphlets were removed only the day before the opening ceremony at the demand of the IOC. Alpine skiing, which includes downhill and slalom, was included for the first time – leading to a major upset when the IOC ruled that ski instructors could not take part because they were professionals. Austrian and Swiss skiers boycotted the events in protest.

When the Olympics resumed after the war, the **1948** winter events were again held in **St Moritz**, from 30 January to 8 February. With Europe still suffering from critical shortages, training facilities were poor and competitions suffered from a daily currency allowance of five Swiss francs. Britain, host to the Summer Games later that year, sent sixty athletes but won only two bronze medals. Germany and Japan were not invited. The Soviet Union did not enter.

The **1952** Games in **Olso** were more successful. A record thirty nations took part, including Germany and Japan. Flags flew at half mast at the opening ceremony after the death of King George VI only a week earlier. Britain's Jeanette Altwegg triumphed in figure skating. The host nation led the medals table, with speed skater Hjalmar Andersen winning three golds.

The **1956** Winter Olympics in **Cortina**, Italy, were the first in which the Soviet Union took part – and ended up winning more medals than any other nation. That was largely down to the Soviet defiance of amateur status, their athletes receiving state support and professional training. In the Alpine events Austrian skier Toni Sailer, the so-called 'Kitzbuhel Cannonball', easily won his record three gold medals. Some events were hampered by lack of snow, which had to be replaced with an artificial covering by the Italian army.

Squaw Valley, California, a minor ski resort with only one hotel and one chairlift, was the unexpected choice of venue for the **1960** Winter Games. It was a triumph of marketing over substance for the Americans. Walt Disney was put in charge of the pageantry for the opening and closing ceremonies and staged an extravaganza in true Hollywood style. A purpose-built village kept the athletes happy. The US upset Canada and Russia to win the ice hockey. The biathlon made its debut. But bobsled was omitted when organisers refused to build a track because only nine countries entered for the event.

Innsbruck, which had lost out by a couple of votes to Squaw Valley, was a fitting choice for **1964** – although the mildest February in living memory meant that the Austrian army had to ferry in thousands of blocks of ice. In the bobsled Tony Nash and Robin Dixon won Britain's only gold. French sisters Christine and Marielle Goitschel finished first and second in two skiing events. And Russian speed skater Lydia Skoblikova became the first athlete to win four golds.

France's President Charles de Gaulle opened the **1968** tenth Winter Olympics at **Grenoble** in a specially built stadium holding 60,000 spectators. It was an all-round triumph for the host nation as Jean-

Claude Killy raced to a skiing golden treble in downhill, slalom and giant slalom – despite a claim of cheating by Austrian rival Karl Schranz. West and East Germany entered separately. East German women competing in the luge finished first, second and fourth but all were disqualified for heating their runners. East German skier Ralph Poehland was not allowed to compete, having defected to the West a month earlier.

Rows over professionalism came to a dramatic head at the **1972** Winter Games in **Sapporo**, Japan. Austria's most famed ski star, Karl Schranz, who had allowed his name to be used for advertising purposes, was barred by the IOC, causing several countries to threaten a boycott. Austria did pull out but re-entered at the request of Schranz himself. In protest at the professional nature of the Soviets, the Canadian ice hockey team withdrew from the event.

In **1976** the Games returned to **Innsbruck** after the residents of the first-chosen host city, Denver, Colorado, refused to finance it. It was a happy second choice, for the Tyrolean town re-used its 1964 facilities to great effect. John Curry's awesome figure skating won a gold for Britain. Austrian local hero Franz Klammer won a popular gold in the Alpine downhill skiing.

The **1980** Games returned to **Lake Placid** and, although the sporting aspects were successful, the organisation was an embarrassing disaster for the American hosts. Many tickets remained unsold even though fans had been desperate to purchase them. And when those with tickets turned up the transport system was unable to cope with the traffic. Taiwan boycotted the Games after the IOC ruled that the country was not allowed to call itself 'Republic of China'. Mainland China itself took part for the first time. The Soviet Union dominated with ten gold medals.

The astonishing pairing of Britain's Jayne Torvill and Christopher Dean created the most memorable moments of the 1984 Winter Games at Sarajevo, then part of communist Yugoslavia. Their 'sixes across the board' performance in ice dance stole the show in a feat that has never been matched. In speed skating, Canada's Gaetan Boucher and East Germany's Karin Enke each won two gold medals, the East German women taking all but three out of the twelve medals in the sport. Katarina Witt, an eighteen-year-old East German, took the figure skating crown. Weather disrupted the skiing but Finland's Marja-Liisa Hamalainen won all three individual cross-country races for women.

Alberta's mild 'Chinook Wind' disrupted the games in **Calgary** in **1988**. Star of the spectacular ski jumping events was Matti Nykunen, again inevitably nicknamed the 'Flying Finn', who won all three ski jump golds. It was Britain's bespectacled Eddie 'The Eagle' Edwards who gained notoriety in this dangerous event. Edwards – rather like the national bobsled team of sunny Jamaica – entered the Games with little experience but gathered mocking media attention, resulting in stricter qualification rules for later Games. Rather more charismatic was Italy's Alberto Tomba, who became a global star with gold in the slalom and giant slalom. Katarina Witt of East Germany successfully defended her figure skating title.

The year **1992** was the last in which the Winter and Summer Games coincided. The decision to alter the schedule had been taken by the IOC six years earlier in response to concerns over increasing costs and complicated logistics.

The opening and closing ceremonies and some of the skating took place in the French mountain resort of **Albertville** while the rest of the events were held in surrounding villages, including fashionable **Meribel** and **Val d'Isere**. Several former Soviet republics entered the Games, along with a rebranded unified Germany team, which moved to the top of the medals table edging out the ex-Soviet states. Italy's Alberto Tomba, nicknamed 'La Bomba', created what was termed 'Bomba-mania' when he became the first Alpine skier to win the same gold medal twice, matching his victory in the giant slalom four years earlier.

Instead of being held in the same year, the Winter Games were now to be held two years after the Summer Games. So **1994** saw **Lillehammer**, Norway, play host. The arrival of more ex-Soviet states helped boost the entries to sixty-seven counties. Nevertheless, Russia won the most events, while Norway collected the most medals. Italy's Manuela Di Centa and Russia's Lyubov Yegorova dominated women's cross-country skiing, taking five and four medals respectively. On the ice, events were overshadowed by American figure skater Tonya Harding's implication in a conspiracy to injure rival Nancy Kerrigan only a month before the Games. In Lillehammer Kerrigan took silver while Harding finished eighth. These Games also saw the introduction of stricter qualifying rules, reducing the number of under-performing entrants from warmer countries. The IOC belatedly recognised the inevitability of sponsorship and changed the rules to permit professionals to reapply for amateur status. This allowed Torvill and Dean to perform again after an absence of a decade. But they took home 'only' a bronze medal.

The **Nagano** Games in Japan in **1998** were the second Winter Olympics in the new schedule. Snowboarding and women's ice hockey made their debut and curling returned for the first time since the inaugural Games. National Hockey League players were allowed to participate in the men's event. Norway's Bjorn Daehlie won three gold medals in cross-country skiing, adding to a tally that made him the highest-winning Winter Olympian. And American fifteen-year-old Tara Lipinski became the youngest individual champion when she took gold in the individual figure skating.

The USA hosted the **2002** Games in **Salt Lake City**, where Norway led with thirteen gold medals, four of which went to Ole Einar Bjoerndalen in the biathlon. Croatia's Janica Kostelic took gold in slalom, giant slalom and the combined, as well as silver in the skiing super-G. Britain won a rare gold thanks to Rhona Martin and her team's curling prowess. However, doping offences saw three cross-country skiers excluded from the Games on the final day. Johann Muehlegg, representing Spain, and Russia's Olga Danilova and Larissa Lazutina failed out-of-competition tests but all three retained the medals they had won earlier. IOC president Jaques Rogge said: "They may technically be champions but I question their moral authority." Since the Games took place in the wake of the 9/11 attacks on New York, Rogge also used his closing address to praise Salt Lake City's security for ensuring a safe venue for athletes and spectators. "You have reassured us that people from all countries can live peacefully together," he said.

There was a less enthusiastic interest by the hosts of the **2006** Games in **Turin**, highlighted by the non appearance of Italian prime minister Silvio Berlusconi at the opening ceremony. The Games suffered low spectator attendance, delays in Alpine events due to poor weather and, dramatically, doping problems. Italian police raided the Austrian athletes' quarters in search of evidence of drug-taking because of suspicions over their biathlon coach Walter Mayer, who had been banned from all Olympic events until 2010 due to previous doping convictions. The verdict on all ten tested Austrian athletes proved negative but Russian Olga Medvedtseva was stripped of her silver medal in the 15 kilometre biathlon event after testing positive and Brazilian bobsled competitor Armando dos Santos was ejected from the Games after a preventive anti-doping test came back positive.

The United States team captured twenty-five medals, its second-highest total ever in the Winter Games and good for second place in the medal count behind Germany. South Korea won ten medals in the short-track speed skating, with three golds in women's for Sun-Yu Jin and another three in men's for Hyun-Soo Ahn. Shelley Rudman took Britain's only medal: a silver in the skeleton bobsled.

Just hours before the opening ceremony of the **2010** Games in Canada, Nodar Kumaritashvili, a Georgian luge slider, was killed during training. Although this tragic event was to overshadow the Games, **Vancouver** and **Whistler**, which played host, still managed to organise a memorable two weeks of winter sports. With fourteen golds, Canada broke the record for the most medals won at a single Winter Olympics although, with a total of thirty-seven, the US won the most medals overall. There was success for Team GB thanks to twenty-seven-year-old Amy Williams who won Britain's first solo Winter Olympics gold for thirty years with victory in the women's skeleton. Norway's Marit Bjoergen triumphed with three golds in three separate skiing events: the sprint, 15 kilometre combined event and the 4 x 5 kilometre relay race.

For the first time both the men's and women's ice hockey were played on the narrower NHL-sized rink, which caused concern amongst the European countries as they felt it gave North American players an advantage. The most exciting innovation was ski-cross, an irresistibly simple sport described irreverently as "sending four crazy skiers together along a bumpy twisting downhill course and seeing who survives". The first gold in that event was won by Michael Schmid of Switzerland

The packed streets, full venues and festive mood gave the province of British Columbia the spirit required to make these Winter Games a major success – a high standard to match for the organisers of the next Winter Olympics, to be held beside the Black Sea at Sochi, Russia, in 2014.

CHAPTER 19

The Paralympic Games

The Paralympic Games, which are now held immediately after the Winter and Summer Olympics, grew out of the fortitude of injured servicemen and women during the World War II. Dr Ludwig Guttmann, a German émigré neurologist at Stoke Mandeville Hospital, Buckinghamshire, hosted a gathering of those veterans with spinal-cord injuries in a sporting contest he called the Wheelchair Games. It began on the same day as the opening of the London Summer Olympics on 29 July 1948.

Four years later it was repeated and was attended by Dutch war veterans – making it the first international competition of its kind. The first such Games open to those other than veterans were held in Rome in 1960, with 400 wheelchair-bound athletes representing twenty-three countries. In Montreal in 1976 the Games were opened to entrants with different disabilities, swelling the numbers to 1,600.

The first winter games of their kind were held in Sweden in 1976. But it was not until France played host in 1992 that the twin winter events shared the same facilities. The biggest breakthrough came in Seoul when the term 'paralympics' came into being. The 1998 Paralympic Summer Games were held immediately after the regular events and using the same facilities, which set a precedent for future Olympiads.

Thus Dr Guttmann's inspirational Wheelchair Games have grown from modest beginnings to reach the present status of a parallel Olympic spectacle, which in 2012 takes place at the Olympic Park and other venues around the country between 29 August and 9 September. What in 1948 was a meeting of a handful of British war veterans has become, by the measure of the last Olympics in Beijing sixty years later, a contest of skill between about 4,000 athletes from 150 countries.

CHAPTER 20

The Cultural Olympiad

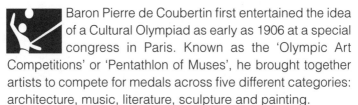Baron Pierre de Coubertin first entertained the idea of a Cultural Olympiad as early as 1906 at a special congress in Paris. Known as the 'Olympic Art Competitions' or 'Pentathlon of Muses', he brought together artists to compete for medals across five different categories: architecture, music, literature, sculpture and painting.

Since its first official appearance during the 1912 Olympics in Stockholm, it has changed considerably. Under IOC rules, a Cultural Olympiad may vary in scale and length from one Olympiad to the next. It has now become a medium for artists to showcase their talents – vitally, 'without competing' – and for the public to take part in creative activities and musical events.

The finale of London's four-year artistic showcase is the London 2012 Festival, a twelve-week nationwide cultural celebration from 21 June to 9 September, featuring leading artists from all over the world.

CHAPTER **21**

The Dream Come True 2012: London

27 July – 12 August

Games of the XXX Olympiad

Countries participating: 204

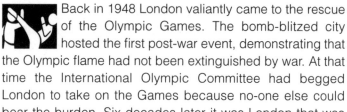Back in 1948 London valiantly came to the rescue of the Olympic Games. The bomb-blitzed city hosted the first post-war event, demonstrating that the Olympic flame had not been extinguished by war. At that time the International Olympic Committee had begged London to take on the Games because no-one else could bear the burden. Six decades later it was London that was doing the pleading – bidding against strong rivals to present a resoundingly successful case for bringing the Olympics back to Britain.

In fact, as we have seen in this brief history of the Olympics, 2012 is the third occasion on which London has played host. And the statistics attached to those three Olympiads – the IV, the XIV and the XXX – reveal how this exposition of international sport has grown beyond what even the most fantastic imaginations could have envisaged when the Games first came to London In 1908.

The Games of the IV Olympiad attracted entries from twenty-two countries, which sent 2,008 athletes, only thirty-seven of them women. By the XIV Olympiad, the number of participating countries had increased to fifty-nine, with the number of athletes also doubled to 4,104, 390 of them women. By comparison, the scale of the Games of the XXX Olympiad is simply mind-boggling…

More than 10,500 Olympic athletes from over 200 countries are expected to compete in 302 events – up from a mere 110 in 1908 and 136 in 1948 – in thirty-four separate venues. They will be witnessed by spectators who have purchased almost nine million tickets, as well as the hundreds of millions of viewers who will follow the events on television around the world. And they will be enthused over and analysed by 20,000 media commentators and cameramen.

The 1908 Games cost £20,000, donations being the major source of revenue, with only twenty-eight per cent of income derived from ticket sales. That price tag was, amazingly, just one millionth of the likely cost of hosting the 2012 Games.

All of which makes the London Games of the XXX Olympiad a monumentally ambitious undertaking, with an investment that underlines how a classical meeting of amateur sportsmen has become the multi-billion-pound greatest show on earth.

London was given just six years to prepare for this brave venture after it won its bid to host the Games through four rounds of voting by members of the International Olympic Committee at the 117th IOC Session in Singapore. The result was announced on 6 July 2005, when London, having overtaken closest rivals New York, Moscow and Madrid, finally pipped Paris to the post in the ultimate ballot.

Then the real race began – led by one of Britain's most famous athletes, Olympic runner turned politician Sebastian Coe, now enobled as Lord Coe. He chaired the London Organising Committee for the Olympic Games (LOCOG), newly formed to implement and stage the entire spectacle. Later, the Olympic Delivery Authority (ODA) was constituted to oversee construction of infrastructure and venues. At Lord Coe's first board meeting in October 2005 the committee faced a daunting task to meet the timescale imposed by the primary decisions already made: when and where?

It had been decided that the Games would take place between 27

THE DREAM COME TRUE – 2012: LONDON

July and 12 August – a two-week span in sharp contrast to the six months over which the 1908 Games had been played out. The next decision involved a construction schedule with the tightest of deadlines...

The focus of sporting activity in 2012 is the Olympic Park in east London, which expects 180,000 visitors every day. It includes the Olympic Stadium, Olympic Village, Aquatics Centre, Velodrome and BMX circuit, plus arenas for basketball, handball and hockey – all easily accessible through a network of footbridges and walkways.

To add historic glamour other prestigious venues were chosen for events to be held further afield, such as Wembley Stadium for football, the All-England Club in Wimbledon for tennis, Lord's Cricket Ground for archery and Horse Guards Parade for beach volleyball. Further venues were chosen, from Dorset to Manchester, to host the increasing number of sports and disciplines contested in a modern Olympics. These include Brands Hatch, Kent, for road cycling, Dorney Lake, near Eton, for rowing and canoeing, and Weymouth and Portland National Sailing Academy in Dorset for sailing events.

Construction of the Olympic Park began three months earlier than originally planned, on 22 May 2008, under the auspices of the ODA and its chairman, civil engineer John Armitt. Work began first on the Olympic Stadium, which will be the central focus of the Games, with an estimated four billion people watching the Opening and Closing Ceremonies and the track and field events held there. Witnessing the beginning of the works, the then Prime Minister Gordon Brown said: "The early start to building work on the Olympic Park site is good news, taking us another step closer to 2012 and the regeneration of one of the country's most deprived areas. I have no doubt that the construction of the new permanent venues, infrastructure and transport links within the largest new urban park to be created in Europe for 150 years will be a catalyst for lasting social and economic change in east London."

A range of transport improvements serving the park include an extension to the Docklands Light Railway, increased capacity on the Jubilee Line and the upgrade of Stratford regional station.

The stadium itself, built with steel from Bolton, concrete terraces from Taunton, seats from Luton, turf from Scunthorpe and providing work for 240 British companies and their sub-contractors, is located in the south of the Olympic Park on an 'island' site, surrounded by waterways on three sides. The stadium's capacity during the Games is 80,000, with

25,000 seats in its permanent lower tier and a further 55,000 in a temporary lightweight steel and concrete upper tier that can be removed after the Games.

Lord Coe described the Olympic Stadium as "the jewel in the crown of the Olympic Park", adding: "It will be a fantastic centre-piece for track and field in the summer of 2012 and provide a lasting legacy for athletics in the UK for generations to come." The Mayor of London, Boris Johnson, also waxed lyrical when the Aquatics Centre was completed in 2011, describing the 50-metre pool as "a poem in concrete and steel" and saying that the water looked "good enough to drink – gin clear!"

An estimated 550 athletes will represent the United Kingdom – all of whom are under enormous pressure to match or better the nation's Beijing score and come in third or fourth on the final medal table. The funding body UK Sport acknowledges the need for Team GB to deliver medals in exchange for the £120 million a year in Exchequer and National Lottery backing.

The personal rewards for success among members of Team GB far exceeds anything that even the most celebrated sporting stars of London's two previous Games could have dreamed of. The race has long been on amongst agents to gamble on the stars of the future and sign them up. One such shining hope is heptathlon entrant Jessica Ennis, already a world and European champion. Those team GB athletes, some who entered the Games as virtually unknown, who win gold could be catapulted to fame and fortune – like double-gold swimmer Rebecca Adlington who, as a nineteen-year-old with no sponsors, stormed from nowhere in Beijing in 2008 to become a household name, with endorsement contracts that brought her a small fortune.

So who is paying for all of this? Commercial sponsors, of course, but also television stations, the British taxpayer – and those members of the public lucky enough to obtain tickets. Half a billion pounds is forecast to be raised from the sale of 8.8million tickets, three-quarters of which, ranging from under £20 to over £2,000, went on general sale 500 days ahead of the Games, with those for over-subscribed events being decided by ballot. Of the remaining 2.2 million tickets, roughly half were reserved for the national Olympic committees of each country and half split between sponsors, the IOC, guests and hospitality partners.

Several events were made free, such as the marathon. The organisers also promised that 2.5 million tickets would be available for

£20 and under. A clever idea was for children under 17 to 'pay-your-age' to see some of the early heats, while over-60s could watch the same events for £16.

As London celebrated the twelve-month countdown to the XXX Olympiad in Trafalgar Square on 27 July 2011, Prime Minister David Cameron hailed a "great British story; it's on time and budget". It had always been a somewhat shifting budget, however. At the time he spoke, the project's budgeted cost had risen from an original £2.4 billion to £9.3 billion. But politicians and organisers promised that there would be a payback. Boris Johnson said that, while the 2012 Olympics will not be as dramatic or as supersized as Beijing, they would make the capital the "epicentre of fun in the universe".

With an expected influx of 800,000 visitors, an increase in spending by tourists of £700 million is forecast, while Britons are likely to boost their spending by £40 million. Beyond London, Visa, one of the sponsors, expects a £41 million increase on spending as the country supports the Games. The company forecast "British residents are likely to switch from traditional summer spending to getting into the Olympic spirit by stocking up on supplies and entertaining at home. Supermarkets will be particular beneficiaries of this." Hotels will benefit too, setting aside 40,000 rooms in Central London at below market rate. The British Beer and Pub Association applied to extend licensing hours, hoping for a 'liquid gold' effect.

Early on, the Olympic committees of the competing nations hired some of London's most historic venues, boosting the capital's economy by £120 million. Brazil booked Somerset House, Jamaica Finsbury Park, Italy the QE11 Conference Centre, Germany the Museum of London, Belgium the Inner Temple and Switzerland the Glaziers Hall in the Square Mile.

When Lord Coe won the London Olympic bid he made a pledge to use the events to inspire two million people to take up sport and physical activity. The legacy of the Games, he said, includes sporting, economic, cultural and environmental benefits. To ensure that no 'white elephants' are created in the aftermath of the Games, an Olympic Park Legacy Company was set up in 2009 with the aim of transforming the Olympic Park into one of the largest urban parks created in Europe for more than 150 years.

The Athletes' village will be converted into homes, many available for key workers such as teachers and nurses. Further housing will be built within the Olympic Park site. Riverside housing, shops, restaurants and cafés will provide new amenities. Communities surrounding the park will enjoy access to the open space via a network of canal towpaths, footpaths and cycleways. Some playing fields will be adapted for community use. The world-class sports facilities will be retained for use by sports clubs and the local community as well as elite athletes. Economically the area will be transformed.

But first comes the Games… and the final celebratory event leading up to it: the delivery of the Olympic torch, the conception and design of which carries special significance.

The torch is triangular, inspired by the identification of certain significant multiples of three: the three Olympic values of respect, excellence and friendship; the three words that make the Olympic motto 'Faster, Higher, Stronger'; the fact London has hosted the Olympic Games three times; and the vision for the 2012 Olympics to combine three strands of work – sport, education and culture. Another numerical link, the propitious number eight inherited from the Beijing Games, has been built into the design of the torch, which weighs 800 grammes, stands 800 millimetres tall and has 8,000 perforations. The torch, following its arrival in Britain from Greece on 18 May 2012, passes to the first of 8,000 "inspirational" torch bearers, setting out from Lands End on an 8,000-mile relay route around the length and breadth of the United Kingdom to the outer regions of Scotland, Wales and Ireland, before finally arriving at the Olympic Stadium on 27 July 2012.

"The flame will shine a light across the nation's regions," said Lord Coe, the man who, more than any other, brought these Games to London. Since his inspirational speech to the IOC in Singapore in 2005, he has overseen the frenetic years of preparation and, as the countdown for the 2012 Games began, he said he couldn't wait for the moment when the Olympic Flame is lit in the Olympic Stadium. As he put it: "This means more to me than winning a gold medal."